SPREADING
THE WEALTH

SPREADING
THE WEALTH

HOW OBAMA IS
ROBBING THE SUBURBS
TO PAY FOR THE CITIES

STANLEY KURTZ

SENTINEL

SENTINEL
Published by the Penguin Group
Penguin Group (USA) Inc., 375 Hudson Street, New York, New York 10014, U.S.A.
Penguin Group (Canada), 90 Eglinton Avenue East, Suite 700, Toronto, Ontario, Canada M4P 2Y3
(a division of Pearson Penguin Canada Inc.)
Penguin Books Ltd, 80 Strand, London WC2R 0RL, England
Penguin Ireland, 25 St. Stephen's Green, Dublin 2, Ireland (a division of Penguin Books Ltd)
Penguin Books Australia Ltd, 250 Camberwell Road, Camberwell, Victoria 3124, Australia
(a division of Pearson Australia Group Pty Ltd)
Penguin Books India Pvt Ltd, 11 Community Centre, Panchsheel Park, New Delhi – 110 017, India
Penguin Group (NZ), 67 Apollo Drive, Rosedale, Auckland 0632, New Zealand
(a division of Pearson New Zealand Ltd)
Penguin Books (South Africa) (Pty) Ltd, 24 Sturdee Avenue, Rosebank, Johannesburg 2196,
South Africa

Penguin Books Ltd, Registered Offices: 80 Strand, London WC2R 0RL, England

First published in 2012 by Sentinel, a member of Penguin Group (USA) Inc.

10   9   8   7   6   5   4   3   2   1

LIBRARY OF CONGRESS CATALOGING-IN-PUBLICATION DATA
Kurtz, Stanley N.
  Spreading the wealth : how Obama is robbing the suburbs to pay for the cities / Stanley Kurtz.
    p. cm.
  Includes bibliographical references and index.
  ISBN 978-1-59523-092-8
  1. Fiscal policy—United States.   2. Taxation—United States.   3. Urban policy—United
States.   4. Suburbs—United States.   5. Metropolitan government—United States.   6. Obama,
Barack—Political and social views.   7. United States—Politics and government—2009–
I. Title.
  HJ2381.K86 2012
  336.73—dc23   2012018007

Printed in the United States of America

CONTENTS

GLOSSARY

NOTE: The terms, individuals, and organizations described here have been selected because they are of particular importance to the argument and recur throughout. This glossary is by no means designed to cover every organization, individual, or term discussed in the book.

Alinskyite: A word that denotes the hard-left goals and hardball tactics favored by Saul Alinsky, self-proclaimed radical and the founder of modern community organizing. Ideologically, Alinsky is probably best described as a "democratic socialist," although he kept his ideological preferences low key for tactical reasons. Alinsky practiced high-pressure confrontation tactics, pursuing political opponents to their homes, for example. Barack Obama is an expert in Alinsky's techniques, and his organizing mentors at the Gamaliel Foundation and Building One America are among Alinsky's most devoted followers.

Building One America: Founded in 2009 by Obama's longtime community organizing mentor Mike Kruglik, Building One America is a network of community organizations and activist groups backing the regionalist movement's efforts to abolish the suburbs. Building One America enjoys a close working relationship with the Obama White House. The group carries on the antisuburban crusade of Obama's longtime organizing network, the Gamaliel Foundation, under a different name.

David Rusk: A former mayor of Albuquerque, New Mexico, Rusk is a founding thinker of the regionalist movement. He favors the formal annexation by cities of their surrounding suburbs. When that is not possible, Rusk supports steps—like regional tax base sharing and mandatory economic integration—designed to accomplish suburban annexation in practice. Rusk has long served as a "strategic partner," first of the Gamaliel Foundation's regionalist crusade and now of Building One America's regionalist successor campaign. Rusk has also worked directly with the Obama administration to design its Sustainable Communities Initiative.

Economic Integration: A key regionalist goal is to make "economic segregation" every bit as legally and morally unacceptable as racial segregation. Through a combination of discrimination lawsuits and regulations, regionalists hope to force the urban poor into the suburbs, just as they hope to use urban growth boundaries, automobile fees, and regulations to force suburbanites back to the cities. Total economic integration would mean that suburbs as we know them would cease to exist. In effect, economic integration would replace the principle that Americans live where they can afford to buy housing with de facto government residential mandates.

Gamaliel Foundation: In 1986, Obama mentor Gregory "Greg" Galluzzo became the executive director of this liberal housing group and transformed it into a training and consulting network for community organizations. Galluzo worked closely during this period with Barack Obama, who became a Gamaliel trainer and whose first community organization, the Developing Communities Project, affiliated with the Gamaliel network. During the mid-1990s, under the leadership of Galluzzo and Obama's other early mentors, Mike Kruglik and Gerald "Jerry" Kellman, the Gamaliel Foundation made grassroots agitation for the antisuburban regionalist crusade the center of its organizing efforts. As an influential board member at the Woods Fund of Chicago in the mid-1990s, Obama was able to channel substantial foundation funding to Gamaliel as it embraced the regionalist movement. Today, the Gamaliel Foundation's long-standing regionalist organizing efforts are carried on through Building One America, founded by Obama mentor and veteran Gamaliel leader Mike Kruglik.

john powell: Professor of law and director of the Kirwan Institute for the Study of Race and Ethnicity at Ohio State University, powell (who prefers that his name be spelled in lowercase), has been a longtime "strategic partner," first to the Gamaliel Foundation's regionalist crusade and then to Building One America's continuation of that regionalist effort. A proponent of the idea that America suffers from a deep vein of "structural racism," powell is also a board member of the Poverty & Race Research Action Council, which serves as a de facto lobbying arm and think tank for Building One America.

Mike Kruglik: One of Obama's three bosses and trainers during the president's initial community organizing stint in Chicago in the mid-1980s (Kellman and Galluzzo were the other two). Under Galluzzo's leadership, Kruglik, Obama, and Kellman helped establish a training and consulting network for community organizations called the Gamaliel Foundation in 1986. From the mid-1990s, under the leadership of Galluzzo, Kruglik, and Kellman, Gamaliel became the leading grassroots force behind the regionalist movement's crusade to abolish the suburbs. In 2009,

Kruglik became the founding executive director of a community organizing umbrella group called Building One America, which carries on the Gamaliel Foundation's long-standing antisuburban crusade under a new organizational name. Kruglik has remained a friend and colleague of Obama's from the mid-1980s to the present, working with Obama during his U.S. Senate years and coordinating Building One America's activities with the president in the White House today.

Myron Orfield: University of Minnesota law professor and former member of the Minnesota House of Representatives and State Senate, Orfield is a major regionalist thinker. He has long served as a key "strategic partner," first to the Gamaliel Foundation's regionalist crusade and now to Building One America's continuation of Gamaliel's regionalist efforts. Orfield led the legislative coalition that brought regional tax base sharing to Minnesota, the only state where that practice currently exists. He remains the most influential proponent of regional tax base sharing to this day. Orfield has worked closely with the White House on a number of the administration's regionalist initiatives.

Regionalism: One name for a movement that travels under many names, including "metropolitanism," "regional equity," "smart growth," and "antisprawl." Bluntly stated, the goal of regionalism is to abolish the suburbs, ideally by having cities annex surrounding suburban municipalities. Failing that, regionalists focus on a three-pronged strategy to effectively render suburbanites' control of their own municipalities meaningless: 1) redistributing suburban wealth throughout a metropolitan region through "tax base sharing"; 2) urban "growth boundaries" to block the development of rural areas, thereby forcing would-be suburbanites back toward the cities; and 3) "economic integration," that is, forced zoning changes and low-income housing mandates designed to force inner-city residents into the suburbs. Regionalists also back various schemes to break down school district boundaries within a given metropolitan region, thereby redistributing suburban school funding to the cities.

Regional Tax Base Sharing: So far put into practice only in the Minneapolis-St. Paul region, this is a scheme in which the taxes collected by suburbs are effectively redistributed to nearby cities and less well-off suburbs. Each municipality in a region is required to place some portion of its tax revenues in a common pool, which is then distributed to all localities in the region by a mathematical formula geared to population. Regional tax base sharing can be imposed on suburban municipalities by state legislatures. Building One America is organizing local legislators to further this longtime goal of the regionalist movement. Former Minnesota legislator Myron Orfield, father of Minnesota's regional tax base sharing scheme, is a key "strategic partner" of Building One America and periodically advises the Obama administration as well.

PREFACE

Barack Obama wasn't kidding when he told "Joe the Plumber" during campaign 2008 that he wanted to "spread the wealth around." Americans still don't know the half of it. Obama's been saving his biggest surprises for what he hopes will be the second act of his presidency. He's spent a couple of decades working on a plan to change the face of America by redistributing suburban tax money to the cities. Over time the president's program would allow the nation's metropolitan centers to effectively swallow up their surrounding municipalities. To put it bluntly, President Obama would like to abolish the suburbs.

While public attention has been riveted on high-profile congressional battles over the stimulus, health care, and the debt ceiling, Obama has been quietly laying the regulatory groundwork for a profound transformation of American society. The founders would not approve. From the Pilgrim Fathers to the frontier settlers to the post–World War II exodus to the suburbs, Americans have enjoyed the freedom to move and to govern themselves as they have seen fit in their new homes. Yet the spirit of enterprise and self-government that made our country great looks very different to Obama.

The fondest dream of the Chicago-based community organizers who trained Obama was to abolish America's suburbs, which according to their radical philosophy were enclaves of privilege from which the urban poor were unfairly excluded. Obama supported their crusade from its birth and today coordinates White House policy on urban-suburban issues with one of his original organizing mentors, although the public is almost totally unaware of this.

In the eyes of Obama's community organizing colleagues—close followers of Saul Alinsky, the leftist radical who founded the profession—America's suburbs are instruments of bigotry and greed. Moving to a suburb in pursuit of the American dream of an affordable family home and quality, locally controlled schools looks to Obama and his organizing mentors like selfishly refusing to share tax money with the urban poor.

Obama means to fix that with regulations designed to force Americans out of their cars and into high-density urban centers, squeezing the population into a collection of new Manhattans. Obama also aims to force suburbanites to redistribute tax money to nearby cities while effectively merging urban and suburban school districts so as to equalize their funding. If you can afford to move to a suburb at all, there will no longer be a point. In effect America's cities will have swallowed up their suburbs. The result: your freedom of movement, America's tradition of local self-rule, the incentive to better your circumstances, and therefore national prosperity all will have been eroded.

Redistributing suburban money to the cities and upending America's system of local government to get there aren't just one more Obama policy initiative. It's what the president cares about most. Obama has as much as told us so in his famous memoir, *Dreams from My Father*, although no one has thought to look to the book as a guide to the president's antisuburban views. Obama's little-known coordination with his community organizing colleagues on a plan to abolish America's suburbs shows that the president's radical past has never disappeared. There is an unbroken line of continuity from Obama's community organizing roots to his presidency. Obama's supporters in the mainstream press can kick and scream all they like, but "Saul Alinsky radical" is a label that sticks.

Once you understand Obama's plan to undo the suburbs and what it means to him, many of his administration's policies appear in a new light. Redistributing suburban tax money to the cities turns out to be an underlying goal of Obama's signature initiatives of health care reform and economic stimulus. Even seemingly unrelated issues like blocking Boeing's move to South Carolina and the war in Libya are connected by the philosophy that guides Obama's antisuburban crusade, as will be explained in the pages ahead.

Americans have always looked to economic growth, not redistribution, as the key to a better life. Sharing out a shrinking economic pie is a zero-sum game, the path to bitter class warfare. Redistribution kills incentives to the growth that benefits all. Meanwhile the blizzard of regulations Obama would use to undercut the suburbs will kill American freedom and self-government. Yet beneath the public's radar, Obama's plan to undo America's suburbs moves forward. Before you decide whether President Obama deserves a second term, this is a transformative enterprise about which you should hear.

CHAPTER ONE

ABOLISH THE SUBURBS

Mike Kruglik, Barack Obama's boss and trainer during the president's initial community organizing stint in Chicago in the mid-1980s, was huddling with a clutch of high-level community organizers and liberal foundation officials in the Ward Room, a small dining area in the West Wing of the White House. Some in the group were almost giddy with excitement, glancing at the nearby door that leads to the White House Situation Room or hanging out later, taking pictures of one another at the entrance to the West Wing. They knew it had been a historic day, the first time a bold project in community organizing had ever been systematically coordinated with the White House, a White House run by a fellow community organizer no less. This little assemblage of senior community organizers and left-leaning funders was debriefing in the aftermath of a White House conference held earlier that day. The conference had been organized by Kruglik and his new group, Building One America (BOA). It was July 18, 2011.

OVAL OFFICE REUNION

Standing by the West Wing door, a couple of the organizers saw President Obama and his close aide Valerie Jarrett walk by. Jarrett had been scheduled to address Building One America's White House conference but was pulled away at the last minute to work with the president on his high-tension negotiations with Republican congressional leaders over the debt ceiling. Yet Jarrett had been coordinating with Kruglik's group for some time and in fact had been the keynote speaker at the summit that had founded Building One America two years before. While Jarrett's absence from the conference had been a disappointment, Kruglik's forum that day had been addressed by a host of high administration officials, including Transportation Secretary Ray LaHood and the senior presidential adviser Pete Rouse. The conference itself, while organized by Kruglik's Building One America, had been convened at the invitation of the White House.

Now, as Building One America's lead organizers and funders finished their postconference assessment in the West Wing, a White House staffer approached Kruglik and told him that the president would like him to come up to the Oval Office for a visit. From the look of the easy smiles on Obama and Kruglik in the uncaptioned photo of the meeting that appears on the Building One America Web site, it was a happy reunion. Yet surely there were poignant moments as well. After all, it had been just over a quarter century since a wet-behind-the-ears community organizer named Barack Obama had earned his stripes under the tutelage of Kruglik and two other organizing bosses on Chicago's South Side. And now here was Kruglik working on a project designed to fundamentally reshape the contours of American society, acting under the supervision of his former charge.

Not that Obama and Kruglik had been out of contact over the past twenty-five years. On the contrary, they'd been in fairly continuous touch all that time. And now their long political partnership was coming to fruition. Touting Kruglik's Oval Office visit, Building One America's Web site describes it as a discussion between "two community organizers." While we certainly don't know all we'd like to about that meeting, we do know that Kruglik briefed Obama on the lead organizers and financial supporters of Building One America and that Obama expressed his support for Kruglik's ambitious venture.[1]

So what exactly is that venture? What is Building One America trying to accomplish? As stated on its Web site's home page, the group's mission is:

> to stabilize and revitalize communities, reinvigorate local economies and promote regional opportunity through broad-based mobilization, leadership development, and the direct engagement of policy-makers at the state and federal level.[2]

Got that? Don't worry, you weren't supposed to. The longer statement of purpose at the Web site will tell you a bit more.[3] You'll learn that Building One America works for things like "fair school funding," "inclusionary housing," and "regional mobility," although precisely what these things are is not specified. Nor does the project as described as a whole sound particularly ambitious or controversial. The few local press reports on the small-town mayors and other local officials who attended the White House event describe Building One America's goals in similarly vague terms.[4] Kruglik and his colleagues are being every bit as forthcoming here as Alinskyite organizers generally are about their ultimate policy goals—that is to say, not forthcoming at all.

SHELL GAME

Mike Kruglik is the least well known and therefore the least controversial of Barack Obama's three original organizing mentors,
a fact by no means unrelated to Kruglik's role as the founding
executive director of Building One America. Obama's memoir,
Dreams from My Father, disguises the identity of his original
bosses by combining all three men into the single figure of "Marty
Kaufman."[5] The Kaufman of *Dreams* most closely resembles Gerald "Jerry" Kellman, the organizer who first interviewed and
hired Obama and who now serves as the director of organizing
for the home branch in Metro Chicago of the Gamaliel Foundation, the national organizing network that Obama himself helped
found along with his three original mentors some twenty-five
years ago. Unlike Kruglik, Kellman was all over the media during
and after campaign 2008, covering for Obama by making the
candidate's earliest organizing ventures and his relationship with
Reverend Jeremiah Wright seem a great deal less troubling than
they actually were.[6] A credulous press bought it all.

By far the most controversial of Obama's three original community organizing mentors is Gregory "Greg" Galluzzo. Galluzzo, along with his wife and fellow organizer, Mary Gonzales,
in 1980 founded the group United Neighborhood Organization (UNO) of Chicago. While UNO has moderated considerably since Galluzzo's departure around 1987, under his direction
it practiced hardball Alinskyite tactics. The most famous
example—although we don't know precisely which UNO leader
arranged it—was an incident in which protesters trapped Republican U.S. senator Charles Percy in a women's restroom. The
original UNO of Chicago was predominantly composed of Mex-
ican immigrants, a high proportion of them illegal. UNO was

infamous for one particularly troubling action: forcing Chicago to name a school after a group of children revered south of the border for having fought against the American Army during the Mexican-American War. This attempt to name a school after America's enemies was sharply opposed by large sections of Chicago's Hispanic community, many of them U.S. Army veterans. For years Chicago's assimilated Latinos thought of Galluzzo's group as a bunch of crazy radicals.[7]

Shortly after Galluzzo and Kellman left UNO of Chicago, they brought in Kruglik and Obama and formed the Gamaliel Foundation, which eventually grew into a national organizing network. Kruglik went on to serve as the foundation's political director, working directly under Galluzzo for years.[8]

The truth is, Kruglik's Building One America is simply a slightly disguised offshoot of Galluzzo's officially separate Gamaliel Foundation, part of a well-honed Alinskyite shell game long played by controversial groups like the Association of Community Organizations for Reform Now (ACORN) to distance themselves from politically delicate and adventurous projects.[9] Back in late 2007, when Obama made his breakthrough at the Iowa caucuses with the help of his old community organizing buddies, he threw his arm around Greg Galluzzo and promised to publicly credit his victory to Galluzzo's organizing mentorship.[10] That was before the details of Obama's Alinskyite past and Galluzzo's own radical history became known. Now Galluzzo complains of being demonized: "I always thought I was doing good work, noble work. Now, shit, I'm seen as a diabolical person."[11] Galluzzo's anything but angelic techniques of polarization and disguise are used by Kruglik's Building One America to this day. Now, however, Galluzzo knows enough to go low profile. The creation of Building One America was a way of hiding the controversial connection among the Obama White House, the Gamaliel Foundation, and Galluzzo.

What all this means is that President Obama is carrying on the most cherished political project of the three radical Alinskyite organizers who originally hired and trained him and working directly with one of them. The only thing that's changed is that Obama is now in charge. Well, that's actually not quite the only thing that's changed. Building One America may be a semi-stealthy offshoot of Obama's original organizing network, yet there's something decidedly novel about this group. Whereas Obama's community organizing colleagues in the Gamaliel Foundation generally work through left-leaning religious congregations, Building One America organizes local elected officials as well as church groups.[12] That is highly unusual.

As a rule, Alinskyites organize the public to put pressure on politicians to spend money. Building One America, on the other hand, is doing something completely unprecedented: it organizes not only the religious left but also sympathetic elected officials to put pressure on other elected officials. Once you understand the full dimensions of the scheme (as Building One America hopes you will not), it's clear that this new group intends to take Alinskyite polarization and class warfare to a whole new level.

SPREAD THE WEALTH

So let us ask it again: What is Building One America's real agenda? What bold transformative project has been undertaken by the community organizer in the Oval Office in partnership with his original Chicago organizing mentor?

The real goal of Building One America and of President Obama himself is to abolish America's suburbs.[13] Ideally, this would happen formally with the annexation of entire metropolitan areas by the cities that form their core. The purpose here is to add suburban tax money to the coffers of cities, thereby cutting off the creation of separate local school systems and municipal services. If Building One America's long-term strategy comes to fruition, the widespread annexation of suburbs by cities may someday take place. At present, however, state laws discourage the involuntary annexation of suburbs by nearby cities. So Building One America's fallback position is a kind of informal abolition of America's suburban landscape, the achievement of which requires three key changes:

First, a no-growth boundary line has to be drawn around each metropolitan area, forbidding the purchase of land for uses other than farming. By blocking off the growth of suburbs, this anti-development wall or line, along with a series of accompanying regulations, will press new development back toward the cities and the inner-ring suburbs, forcing large numbers of Americans to abandon their cars and their dreams of freestanding houses with yards while piling them up instead into dense urban high-rises and public transportation.

Second, America will commit itself to forced economic integration. That is, government will try to systematically manage where people live by income level, to discourage people of similar incomes from settling in concentrated numbers in the same areas. New regulations will force builders to include a quota of low-income housing units in any new development, thus effectively dispersing the urban poor throughout a given metropolitan region. The free market in housing will gradually be replaced by government-planned living patterns. Increasingly, local control over zoning and land use regulation will be ceded to federal, state, and regional governments.

Third, America's metropolitan regions will undertake a regime of tax sharing to reduce "fiscal disparities" among different local governments. In other words, even in the absence of formal annexation, suburban tax money will be transferred to cities and lower-income inner ring suburbs.

So by blocking suburban growth and using regulations to force suburbanites back toward the city and inner-city residents out into the suburbs and by compelling suburbs to share their tax money, a kind of de facto abolition of the suburbs can be achieved.

Building One America's leaders claim that regulations designed to force suburbanites back into cities are justified because the suburbs themselves were created by government policies, like the mortgage interest deduction on the federal income tax. That story, common among leftist academics hostile to the suburbs, is mistaken. America's suburbs are an authentic product of citizen choice, and the plan to eliminate them is deeply coercive and thoroughly hostile to our traditions of individual freedom and local self-rule.

Under Building One America's scheme, an entire layer of local government in America can be effectively eliminated and replaced by just a few massive regional governments. In fact the entire pattern of America's unique federalist system is reversed here. Building One America's plan is to use the authority of state legislatures to force this change. Kruglik's group also means to use the power of the federal government, now headed by its close ally Barack Obama, to press the transition on states and localities. We are looking at a kind of ultimate plan for "big government," in which the "littlest" layer of government is for all practical purposes killed off. Instead of keeping initiative at the local level and reserving for successively higher levels of government only such tasks as remain, the center will increasingly remake and control all else.

You can see the difference between this plan and traditional American practice in the contrast between our national motto, E pluribus unum (Out of many, one), which saves a place for the local level, and Building One America, which sounds nice but leaves out the local "many."

The purpose of this proposed revolution in America's governmental and social structure is the redistribution and equalization of income. What remains at least semidisguised in the case of health care reform is painfully obvious here. A regional tax sharing plan dedicated to reducing fiscal disparities is redistributionist on its face. Call it what you will, "socialism," "social democracy," or just "extreme liberalism," Building One America's program is clearly on the heavily redistributionist, far-left edge of Democratic Party politics. This transformative and highly controversial scheme is Building One America's secret and Obama's secret too.

SPLIT THE SUBURBS

Social revolutions like this don't happen without a political plan, and Obama and his allies in Building One America have got one. The idea is to take the suburbs, now the swing constituency in national elections, and divide them against themselves. Obama wants to create a political alliance between cities and older inner-ring suburbs, in effect urging these constituencies to gang up on the bulk of the suburbs in state legislatures to impose regional tax sharing plans on a reluctant middle class.[14]

Building One America's novel attempt to organize local and state-level politicians from inner-ring suburbs—the real purpose of BOA's White House conference—is designed to set up this giant national battle of the future. This will be class warfare on a scale set to dwarf the puny efforts of Occupy Wall Street. And you can be certain Obama's class warfare of the future will raid the wallets of a whole lot more than just the wealthiest "1 percent" of us. The real targets are the inhabitants of America's suburbs.

So Obama's long-term goal is to build a new and permanent Democratic majority on the promise of regional income redistribution. But to succeed, this movement will have to change our ideals in fundamental ways. It will have to kill off the traditional American dream, the idea of constant striving for a better future, symbolized by the middle-class goal of a rising income and the purchase of a little house with a yard—not to mention the freedom to move where you please, run your life, and govern your town with your neighbors when you get there.

Greg Galluzzo, Obama's mentor and the man who created the grassroots crusade that inspired Building One America, dismisses the American dream as a sham. What really makes Americans move to the suburbs, says Galluzzo, is "racism and greed."[15]

Imagine for a moment what the reaction would be were it discovered that President Obama had been meeting with his controversial former pastor, Jeremiah Wright, or the notorious small "c" communist, Pentagon bomber, and onetime Obama colleague, Bill Ayers at the White House and quietly coordinating with either of them on a redistributionist plan to change the face of American government and society as we know them. How is this any different? Kruglik may be less well known than Wright or Ayers, yet he and his colleagues in the Gamaliel Foundation are every bit as radical and every bit as much a part of the president's questionable past as Ayers and Wright.

Nor was Building One America's July 2011 White House conference an isolated affair. As noted, Valerie Jarrett and the White House have been coordinating with the group since its inception in 2009. High administration officials have been working with Building One America at the group's local meetings as well as in Washington, and the administration has pledged to continue that grassroots cooperation.[16] Kruglik himself has been quietly giving policy advice to the Department of Housing and Urban Development for the past few years.[17]

More broadly, while the Obama administration has downplayed its redistributionist motivations and its most controversial long-term goals, it has been advancing a "regionalist" agenda for years. This is a major and deeply serious presidential initiative. Yet few Americans know a thing about it.

For decades Democratic and Republican presidents alike were virtually required to have an urban policy, the ins and outs of which were widely discussed. It was only after the failure of the War on Poverty was broadly acknowledged during the Reagan years that the public stopped expecting presidents to have an urban policy.[18] But Obama does have an urban policy, and Building One America's agenda is it. It's just that the president would rather you not know this until after he's reelected.

STILL RADICAL

In late October 2011, several months after Building One America's White House conference, Housing and Urban Development Secretary Shaun Donovan addressed a meeting of BOA's state affiliate, Building One Pennsylvania, in Lancaster. There Donovan decried what he called "the tyranny of the zip code," a catchphrase that may someday become a rallying cry for Building One America's radical regionalist agenda. Secretary Donovan repeatedly invoked the president's community organizing background in his speech, noting that "for the first time in history, you have a community organizer . . . sitting in the Oval Office."[19]

Curiously, at the very moment that Obama's HUD secretary was bragging to a radical Alinskyite group with which his department had been cooperating that America now had its first community organizer in the Oval Office, the entirely justified claim by the Republican presidential candidate Newt Gingrich that Obama was a believer in Saul Alinsky radicalism kicked up a controversy among conservatives. While many critics of President Obama were thrilled by Gingrich's remarks, a few (seemingly) pragmatic Republicans were dismayed. Not that they disputed the truth of Gingrich's claim. Their argument instead was that if attacks on Obama's radical Alinskyite roots had failed to gain traction in 2008, they were unlikely to succeed now. Why not focus instead on what voters really cared about, these cautious conservatives suggested: not Obama's radical past, but his four years of failed presidential policies in the here and now?[20]

The problem with this conservative debate over the political significance of Obama's radical Alinskyite past is that it completely ignores his radical Alinskyite *present*. The truly important political critique of President Obama is that right now, this very day, he is using his long-standing Alinskyite alliances and convictions to guide administration policy while keeping his radical goals from the public. The president's political history is an invaluable resource for making sense of these poorly known policies and future plans, of course, but the real problem exists today and tomorrow, not in the past.

We should acknowledge, however, that when it comes to leveling a charge of radicalism against President Obama, conservative pragmatists have a point. While Obama's goals are in fact quite radical, uttering that truth out loud really is a problem. Why is that?

It's true, of course, that the mainstream press favors Obama and habitually protects him from harsh charges. Some members of the media may be taken in by Obama's "postpartisan" veneer while others understand his transformative and decidedly leftist ambitions yet soft-pedal all that so as not to disturb the public. In either case, the result is a defensive shield for the president.

Then there's the elemental respect Americans rightly hold for the office of the presidency. An American president is not only a head of government but also the head of state, the embodiment of our nation's power and dignity. Obama conducts himself with an easy grace that befits his high post. So having won the presidency, Obama by just holding that office tends to be protected from harsh-sounding charges.

More than that, something about a claim of presidential radicalism seems off base. Almost by definition, any president who seeks to wield influence—especially if he's running for reelection—has little choice but to appeal to a broad swath of the American public. If political radicals stand at the edges of American politics, the description seems inappropriate to a president maneuvering for reelection.

Yet it's just here that the radicalism of Obama's hidden regionalist agenda proves itself. It isn't just that Obama keeps his anti-suburban plans below the public radar because they confirm virtually everything his conservative critics have ever claimed about him. The deeper problem is that were the full truth about Obama's regionalist agenda to come out, it would split his electoral coalition. Obama's regionalist plans are nothing less than a direct attack on large sections of his own middle-class supporters. It's true that over the very long term Obama and his Alinskyite allies in Building One America hope to reshape American attitudes, thereby creating a new and dominant redistributionist coalition of the left. In the short term, however, were Obama's plans to be revealed, they would show him to be substantially to the left of even his own party's center of gravity.

The history of Kruglik's long campaign for regionalism, extending back to his years with the Gamaliel Foundation, confirms this. Time after time, even after showing an initial receptiveness to his plans, Kruglik's mainstream liberal allies learned what Gamaliel's real agenda was, then ran screaming the other way. The same thing would happen to Obama were the full truth about his own radical regionalist goals to emerge too soon.

In November 2011 the political commentator Thomas Edsall caused a stir with a column in the *New York Times* arguing that

President Obama was going to run for reelection by assembling a new progressive coalition that would largely "abandon the white working class."[21] While the notion that Obama might consciously write off white working-class voters sparked wide discussion, Edsall's claim that Obama's new coalition would consist of "young people, Hispanics, unmarried women, and affluent suburbanites" went virtually unnoticed and uncommented upon.

What about those "affluent suburbanites"? The political experts cited by Edsall believe that socially liberal affluent suburbanites will increasingly align themselves with the Democratic Party.[22] But what if the affluent suburbanites at the core of Obama's coalition learned that the president would be pleased to see their communities swallowed up by nearby cities? What if these suburbanites woke up to the fact that Obama's long-term plan was to raid their wallets and "spread their wealth around" so as to remove any fiscal disparities within the nation's metropolitan regions? At that point Obama's new progressive coalition could fall apart. It's been known since 2008 that Barack Obama has little love for white working-class voters who "bitterly cling" to their guns and Bibles. The real news is that Obama's no fan of America's middle-class suburbs either.

The surprises don't end there. Even many of the Hispanics and African Americans at the heart of Obama's new progressive coalition would be dismayed to learn of Obama's regionalist plans. You might think the opposite would be true. While Obama's ultimate interest is in wealth redistribution across the board, surely at least a part of the motivation for his regionalist policies is to remove fiscal disparities between relatively poor minorities and other Americans. While Obama and his Alinskyite allies in Building One America may see things that way, the regionalist agenda has always been controversial among minorities themselves.

As African Americans have made up an increasingly larger

share of the population of America's cities, they have moved into high political office and into the urban bureaucracy as well. Attempts to enlarge the powers of regional governments or to have cities actually annex nearby suburbs are viewed by many minorities as a way of diluting their newfound influence within America's cities. Obama's Alinskyite allies attribute that stance to "turf protection."[23] But why aren't minorities allowed to cherish the same traditions of localism and community control that Americans have valued for generations?

The optimistic political interpretation of Obama's regionalist plans is that an alliance of relatively disadvantaged urban and inner-ring suburban politicians will someday tip America's power balance to the left, ushering in income redistribution on a grand scale. The negative view is that the radicalism of these plans, once exposed, will split Obama's own coalition, alienating large sections of the white, black, and Hispanic middle class.

All this helps explain why President Obama has been so reluctant to sketch out his broader, long-term vision for America. Until very recently the left has been frustrated by Obama's failure to use the bully pulpit of the presidency to aggressively proselytize for ideological liberalism. In part the president's reticence stems from a recognition that he governs what is still a center-right country. More than that, Obama's vision is to the left of even many of his own strongest supporters. And this most especially is what has forced him into silence about his long-term plans.

THE MISSING KEY

In and of itself, Obama's support for a movement that seeks the de facto and, ultimately, the formal legal abolition of the suburbs is important news. This is a crusade at least on a par in its long-term ambitions with Obama's health care reform, his cap and

trade proposals, his stimulus, and his banking law. Yet the importance of Obama's heretofore little-known regionalist ambitions
goes beyond this single policy area. To a surprising degree,
Obama's regionalist vision provides the missing link that connects
his radical political past to his present, exposing in the process the
broader rationale behind many seemingly unrelated policy initiatives. A number of Obama's policies can be understood as direct
or indirect attempts to address urban issues, subtly reconstituting
President Johnson's failed War on Poverty. Obama's commitment
to the regionalist crusade helps make that connection clear.

To put it another way, the plight of the city in its (supposed)
struggle with the suburbs is where Obama's heart is. This is what
he most cares about. We know this because he has told us so,
although few have properly noticed or grasped his message.
Obama's famous memoir, *Dreams from My Father*, can easily be
read as a story of city versus suburb. Many of the most widely
discussed incidents in the book, from the story of Obama's anti-
apartheid activism to his reminiscences of Marxist professors to
his conversion by Jeremiah Wright's sermon on the audacity of
hope, are wrapped around stories of tension between city and
suburb. We'll need to go back to Obama's own life and writings
to understand just how important the regionalist crusade really is
to this president. To a remarkable degree, we can reconstruct
Obama's stunningly personal take on this issue by considering
anew his own words. Oddly, the policy Obama cares about most
is the one the public knows least.

President Obama has very effectively kept this issue under the
radar. It would have been easy enough to foreground his regionalist crusade in a presidential speech, a news conference, or a state
of the union address. That would have quickly injected this battle
into public debate. Clearly, however, Obama wanted to avoid
that, although the regionalist crusade is unquestionably of great
importance to him.

The writings of Obama's regionalist allies are filled with ac-knowledgments of the politically explosive nature of their quest. Those same writings are awash in surprisingly frank acknowledg-ments of the necessity of both stealth and patient incrementalism to the regionalist crusade. The regionalist literature, much of it written by Obama's longtime mentors and advisers or their close associates, opens a window onto the president's strategic thinking on this subject and many others as well.

A moment ago, when I asked how the public might react to news that Bill Ayers or Jeremiah Wright had been collaborating with Obama on ambitious far-left policy initiatives, it might have seemed as though this prospect, at least, was a bridge too far for the president. In the literal sense that may be true. Mike Kruglik is less known and less notorious than Ayers and Wright, so a partnership with him can be risked, although Obama's collabora-tion with Kruglik is no less disturbing than his ties to Wright and Ayers, once you realize what's going on. And when you under-stand the full implications of Obama's regionalist policies, it's clear as well that the spirits of Ayers and Wright continue to haunt this administration.

Reverend Wright has been a longtime partner of the Gamaliel Foundation in its regionalist crusade (as ACORN has been as well, by the way).[24] More important, Wright's controversial at-tacks on "middle classness" have everything to do with Obama's regionalist policies.

Bill Ayers worked for years on K–12 education with Obama, and it turns out that Obama's troubling and little-discussed second-term education plans give all the signs of being a contin-uation of both his work with Ayers and his broader regionalist agenda.

Obama's complex dance with Occupy Wall Street, a move-ment he very arguably stirred up with his class warfare rhetoric, shows up in a fascinating new light when seen through the lens of the theories and tactics of the president's old organizing buddies in the regionalist movement.

The argument that Obama's long-term plans for health care reform are really a kind of stealthy creep toward a government-run single-payer system is considerably strengthened when set beside the example of the president's regionalist policies.

Efforts by Obama's National Labor Relations Board to block Boeing's move from Washington State to South Carolina make perfect sense when seen in the light of the regionalist gospel.

The claim that Obama's real model for America is European social democracy is greatly strengthened by the fact that America's regionalists take their cue from Europe. Indeed, in fascinating ways, the crisis of the European Union repeats many of the problems and dynamics of American regionalism. Europe's social democrats (who also often call themselves socialists) have an impulse to move government up to successively higher levels, undercutting local democratic traditions and relying on rule by leftist technocrats in the process. In the end Obama's regionalist plans repeat, in an American context, many of the problems of governmental scale that have already done in the unfortunate Europeans.

Perhaps most important, echoing the rallying cry of Occupy Wall Street, Obama has framed his bid for reelection as an appeal to America's middle class to join him in his battles against the wealthiest 1 percent. Yet Obama's support for a regionalist movement determined to force a massive redistribution of wealth away from the suburbs reveals that his real financial target is America's middle class, many of them his own supporters. The American public has a right to know the truth about Obama's largely hidden second-term plans before they go to the polls in 2012. Conveying that truth is the most important task of *Spreading the Wealth*.

We'll look into all the wider policy implications of Obama's regionalist crusade listed above and more in the final chapter of this book. Let us first, however, strengthen our hold on the regionalist key that opens a new perspective on so much else. We'll trace the history and explore the character of America's regionalist movement in chapters 2 and 3, very much including its place in the Obama administration. Chapter 4 recovers the lost history of the founder of community organizing, Saul Alinsky, and shows how Obama carries on Alinsky's project through his regionalist campaign and in many other ways. Then we'll plumb the depths of Obama's own life and writings in chapter 5, to discover why the contest of city and suburb stands so close to his heart. In chapter 6 we'll assess the merits of the regionalist case. Chapter 7 penetrates the Obama administration's little-known but troubling education policies to find the regionalist purpose behind them. Chapter 8 returns, as promised, to the big picture, assessing a whole range of Obama administration policies in light of all that we will have learned about his regionalist crusade. The Conclusion recapitulates the core argument of the book.

We'll learn that the young Barack Obama struggled to repudiate his inner suburbanite as a way of sharing in big-city cool. And although it remains almost totally unknown to the public, a great deal of Obama's early political career was devoted to the goal of abolishing America's suburbs, a project he undertook in close collaboration with his Alinskyite organizing mentors. Today the Obama administration has in place a series of little-known policies designed to undermine the suburbs by effectively merging them with the cities. The president, in short, has been laying the groundwork for a profound transformation of American society although the public has barely been told.

When Obama's already substantial collaboration with his Alinskyite colleagues expands still further in a possible second term, the radically redistributive effort to undercut America's suburbs will go public. At that point Obama's federal government will join hands with Kruglik's grassroots movement to put the squeeze on state legislatures across the country to force tax sharing on the suburbs. Obama's little-known plans to nationalize America's school system will also kick in during a second term and will serve as the lever for a massive transfer of wealth from America's suburban school districts to the cities.

As all this emerges, it will grow increasingly evident that Obama's signature policies of health care reform, the stimulus, and other regulatory changes have in significant part been designed to advance a large-scale redistribution of wealth from America's suburbs to its cities.

If this disturbs you, the best way to prevent it is to learn about it now, before it's too late to take action in the voting booth. So if a sweeping redistributive plan to undermine America's system of local government is not your cup of tea, read on.

CHAPTER TWO

MANHATTANIZING AMERICA

"The days where we're just building sprawl forever, those days are over." So said President Obama just three weeks after his inauguration.[1] To a great many American families, what Obama calls sprawl is really the dream of an affordable home and a yard for the kids to play in. Yet the president's comment signaled determination to channel future development away from the suburbs.

That none-too-subtle knock on sprawl was a rare unguarded indication from Obama of his plans to transform America's physical and political landscape. It came during an unscripted moment at a town hall meeting in Florida. It also rankled some folks, who wondered what business it was of a president to decide how or where Americans should live.[2] Since then Obama has been careful to steer clear of such bald statements.

Yet Obama's plans for the suburbs are a critically important, if little-recognized, element of his administration's policies. While the president's support for Building One America reveals the radical side of his regionalist vision, Obama's alliance with his organizing mentors is very much a part of his administration's broader and already well-established antisuburban—that is, regionalist—agenda.

Members of Obama's cabinet, for example, have been fairly adventurous on the topic of suburbs. Transportation Secretary Ray LaHood has promised to fight suburban sprawl by finding ways to "coerce people out of their cars."[3] Secretary of Housing and Urban Development Shaun Donovan has declared: "We've reached the limits of suburban development: people are beginning to vote with their feet and come back to the central cities."[4]

Donovan is wrong about that. Americans still show a preference for detached single-family houses and commuting by car.[5] Yet from the president on down, the Obama administration likes to claim that the heyday of the suburbs has passed. It's easier to say that the suburbs' days are over, of course, than to admit, as Secretary LaHood did under the pressure of questioning, that the administration is bent on coercion—that is, forcing Americans to change their way of life.

SHHHH!

The president has had more to say about America's cities and suburbs than that quick, unguarded remark in Florida. Before penetrating the fog of ObamaSpeak, however, let's take in the sounds of silence. Why haven't we heard more about the Obama administration's plans for the suburbs? In part, of course, controversies over the stimulus, Obamacare, and unemployment have taken center stage. Still, there's more to the silence than that. Although Obama has been reluctant to declare his bold plans to change the way Americans live, put an ear to the ground, and you just might hear the distant rumble of an oncoming regional revolution. A quick consideration of the history of urban policy will make sense of the quiet and the roar.

Lyndon Johnson's expensive and largely unsuccessful War on Poverty is the foundation of modern urban policy. In the wake of Johnson's efforts, presidents felt the need to have a more or less explicit urban agenda. President Nixon placed his urban team under the supervision of the prominent Democratic intellectual Daniel Patrick Moynihan. President Carter had an urban plan as well although political infighting and economic troubles meant it never truly got off the ground.[6]

In general, Democrats in Congress and the presidency have tried to direct heavy government funding to poor neighborhoods in big cities. As congressional representation from America's suburbs has grown, however, that sort of targeting has been curtailed in favor of block grants made available to most parts of the country (block grants are lump sums given to states or localities to target problems such as education or housing, with the recipient state or locality controlling how the money is spent). When, on top of this change, it became evident that the War on Poverty had largely failed to help the very people it was meant to benefit, the Reagan administration cut back on the whole effort. George H. W. Bush continued Reagan's cutbacks, while George W. Bush offered some additional block grants to the states.

In effect, in the post-Reagan era, presidents simply stopped having an explicit urban policy. That's why the press doesn't talk about it. Close observers know better, however. According to the urban policy experts Bernard Ross and Myron Levine, President Clinton "practiced a stealth urban policy, pursuing urban goals through 'nonurban' means."[7] Clinton, they say, "did not talk explicitly about cities."[8] Instead he put forward policies on crime, education, and other areas, many of which were consciously directed toward cities, even if he never said so. The most momentous such policy was Clinton's effort to loosen credit standards and gin up the subprime mortgage industry as a way of spreading homeownership to impoverished inner cities. Urged on by radical community organizations like ACORN, that policy laid the foundations of our current economic crisis, leaving high and dry the very home buyers it was designed to help.[9] Even stealthy urban policies can have hugely harmful effects.

According to Ross and Levine, President Obama has followed Clinton's "pragmatic" strategy, refusing to announce an explicit national urban policy while creating one anyway on the sly. The Brown University sociologist Hilary Silver, who convened a symposium of left-leaning policy wonks to figure out whether Obama had an urban policy at all, concluded that the administration does in fact have what she calls a stealth urban policy buried in places like the stimulus, support for Fannie and Freddie, and above all the new emphasis on regionalism.[10]

It's not just suspicious conservatives, then, but Obama's own liberal supporters who've been claiming he has an urban policy that he's not fully owning up to. Even First Lady Michelle Obama seems to have made the point. The columnist and prominent Obama cheerleader Jonathan Alter tells the following story in *The Promise*, his chronicle of the president's first year:

> A congressman approached the first lady at a White House reception after the [stimulus] bill's passage and told her the stimulus was the best antipoverty bill in a generation. Her reaction was "Shhhh!" The White House didn't want the public thinking that Obama had achieved long-sought public policy objectives under the guise of merely stimulating the economy, even though that's exactly what had happened.[11]

Alter is criticizing Obama from the left, arguing that the president should have accepted the short-term political risk of honesty for the sake of gaining long-term credit for a major policy reversal, a return to exactly the sort of big-government antipoverty programs once ended by Ronald Reagan. Robert Rector and Katherine Bradley of the conservative Heritage Foundation argue that Obama's stimulus effectively abolished welfare reform as famously enacted in 1996 although few have attended to their analysis.[12] We can wonder today whether the little-known Great Society elements of the stimulus might help explain its economic failure. Yet the larger point is that Obama's friends and supporters, including even the first lady, have acknowledged that he's been pursuing a stealthy urban agenda.

Obama is doing much more, however, than quietly reviving the old War on Poverty. Ultimately his plans go far beyond the old drive to channel federal money to impoverished urban neighborhoods although that's certainly part of his program. In the end Obama means to radically reshape the United States, not just a few urban neighborhoods.

OBAMA SPEAKS

So the first layer of protection for Obama's urban policy is that few people know that he's even got one. The president says little about urban affairs per se. Obama's second layer of protection is the misleading language game he uses on those rare occasions when he does speak about urban affairs. Whenever Obama talks about cities, he emphasizes that he's interested not just in cities but in entire metropolitan regions, suburbs included. The problem is that Obama's actual interest in the suburbs lies in redistributing their tax money to the cities, stripping suburban municipalities of their right to self-rule, and forcing suburbanites to move back to town.

"Regionalism" is actually just a fancy word for a thoroughly antisuburban agenda. Obama never explains the real goals of the regionalist movement, of course. So when he says he is really very interested in the economic health of "regions," it sounds as though he cares equally about cities and suburbs. In reality it means that Obama is aiming to fleece suburbanites and hand their hard-earned income over to the cities.

In short, the president's incantation of the regionalist mantra has allowed him to pull off the masterstroke of appearing to care about both city and suburb when the real point of his policy is to transfer suburban resources to cities. Saying, "I care about regions," sounds like a policy of universal love when it is actually a policy of redistributive favoritism toward the cities. Obama gets to promote the interests of cities (and a few relatively impoverished inner-ring suburbs) at the expense of the rest of the country, even as his language mistakenly suggests that he's surrendered the dream of another War on Poverty.

Obama has given only two significant speeches on urban issues. The first was to the U.S. Conference of Mayors during campaign 2008. That address called for a break with outdated urban agendas and demanded more attention to "our growing metro areas."[13] The *New York Times* portrayed the speech as an effort to focus on "metropolitan growth rather than chiefly on inner-city crime and poverty."[14]

Not quite. The foundation of Obama's metropolitan policy is actually the belief that inner-city crime and poverty are caused by suburban growth. That's what Obama's community organizing mentors—the leaders of the Gamaliel Foundation and Building One America—believe, and that's why Obama means to put a stop to what he calls suburban sprawl. The president's supposed concern for "metropolitan growth" is more like concerned *opposition*.

Obama's only serious public foray into urban issues as president came at a Brookings Institution conference on urban and metropolitan policy ("metropolitan policy" is another term for "regionalism"). The conference, held in July 2009, was attended by numerous cabinet secretaries and high administration officials.[15]

Hilary Silver, the sociologist who described what she calls Obama's stealth urban policy, said of that address: "even the experts can be excused for missing [the 2009 Brookings] speech that Obama gave on urban affairs, since press coverage of it was minimal."[16] Then Silver added: "But there is another reason why urbanists gave that speech little attention. The president repeatedly referred to 'cities and metropolitan areas' in a single breath. Much as he has taken pains to avoid singling out the 'special' concerns of African-Americans, it appears he will not target cities per se. Rather, by referring to 'metropolitan areas' of one million or more in population, he can take in 80 percent of the population."[17]

The Fordham University political scientist Paul Kantor, who evidently favors a redistributionist urban policy, makes a similar point. According to Kantor, Obama's speeches "about economic development are devoted to redefining 'urban' to mean metropolitan regions and avoid inner-city connotations."[18] Kantor hopes that this rhetorical strategy will allow Obama to broaden the political coalition in support of federal aid to cities, but he also worries that the very breadth of the coalition will limit Obama's ability to redistribute tax money. (What Kantor, along with just about everybody else, has missed is that Obama is aware of this barrier to his redistributive plans and hopes to use Building One America to remove it.)

Silver and Kantor may also be implying that Obama's metropolitan policy serves as a cover for aid to African Americans. Obama does care a great deal for the welfare of the African American community, of course. For Obama, however, this game is really about class. The president is a man of the left, and his interest in pushing redistributive schemes designed to wipe out differences of class—regardless of ethnicity or race—is completely sincere, if misguided. Moreover, the regionalist gospel is controversial among many middle-class blacks.

When you read Obama's little-known addresses on metropolitan policy, it's easy to spot yet another reason for the president to downplay this issue. It's impossible for Obama to talk about urban policy without having listeners think back to his days as a community organizer. Obama opened his 2008 address to the U.S. Conference of Mayors by calling his community organizing days in Chicago "the most important experience in my life." He went on to reference several incidents familiar to readers of *Dreams from My Father.* He harked back to his community organizing days again in his 2009 Brookings address, and the experts who write about Obama's urban-metropolitan policy repeatedly touch on his background in community organizing. With Obama's radical Alinskyite past far more controversial today than it was at the start of his first presidential campaign, the topic of urban policy is clearly awkward for him. Supposedly, Obama's Alinskyite radicalism is a relic of a bygone era. Yet a serious look at Obama's "metropolitan" policy gives the lie to that claim.

CHEATIN' COUNTRY FOLKS

What about country folks, by the way? In all this talk of aid to cities and suburbs, somehow small towns and rural areas have gotten lost. That is not by happenstance. It's true that Obama's regionalist policy at least claims to focus on the interests of the 80 percent or so Americans who live in metropolitan areas. The countryside doesn't even rate so much as token inclusion.

Obama is perfectly aware of this delicate political problem. In his Brookings address, just after emphasizing that our metropolitan areas are home to the lion's share of the nation's jobs and economic output, Obama hastened to add that funneling money to these regions would in no way slight rural Americans. This is supposedly because rural areas benefit from the flourishing of nearby metropolitan economies. "Our urban and rural communities," said Obama, "are not independent; they are interdependent."

The fundamental challenge for Democratic presidents and lawmakers is to disproportionately funnel money to their own urban constituencies. Whereas Republican presidents have tended to offer block grants with no strings to the states, Democrats hope to target federal spending to impoverished urban neighborhoods.[19] This is why leading regionalist policy experts, like Bruce Katz of the Brookings Institution, complain of politicians who spread money out evenly to every district "like peanut butter."[20] Of course the real cure for too much peanut butter is a diet. That was President Reagan's approach when he cut federal spending for all programs, whether targeted to cities or not.

But if hundreds of billions of dollars are to be spent, Democrats need to find a rationale for handing the money to their own supporters and holding it back from everyone else. That's where regionalism comes in. Step one is to claim that the American economy rests upon the health of a few key metropolitan regions. That cuts the rural folks out from the start. Step two is to say that our economically critical metropolitan regions can't do well if some of their neighborhoods are doing poorly. The third step is to demand, for the sake of the metropolitan region as a whole and even the outlying countryside that depends on it, that federal aid be funneled disproportionately to impoverished urban neighborhoods. Presto! A policy based on an ideology of redistribution has been dressed up in the language of economic competitiveness. It's all for the good of the economy, say the regionalists, but equalizing incomes is the real goal.

By defining metropolitan regions as the key to the economy, you slight the contributions of rural Americans. Yet it would have been just as easy to draw lines around America's most economically productive areas in such a way as to exclude impoverished inner-city neighborhoods. That may be a bad idea, but it's exactly how Obama has treated America's countryside.

Bruce Katz, the guru of metropolitanism and a key Obama adviser on this issue, along with coauthor Jennifer Bradley, published a piece attacking Sarah Palin in the *New Republic* during the 2008 campaign. The article was titled "Village Idiocy."[21] There Katz and Bradley claimed that Palin doesn't actually come from small-town America at all. That, they said, is because Palin's hometown of Wasilla, Alaska, is nestled in a borough (county) from which a third of workers commute to Anchorage. According to Katz and Bradley, Palin ought to think of herself as a proud member of the Anchorage metropolitan region and should presumably therefore insist upon policies that channel federal money to that city. But what about the two-thirds of workers in Sarah Palin's county who don't commute to Anchorage? And what about the ultimate dependence of our cities on the food, lumber, and oil drawn from the countryside?

Obama's favored metropolitan policy wonks complain about federal aid spread around like peanut butter by vote-hungry politicians, while they claim to offer policies based on "facts," like the measurable contribution of metropolitan regions to our economy.[22] Yet their supposed facts are manipulated in a heads-I-win, tails-you-lose political game. When your constituents are thriving, claim they need federal money because they're the foundation of the economy. When your voters are doing poorly, claim they need federal money because the health of the region depends on even-handed economic development. When somebody else's constituents are doing well, demand that they subsidize your voters. And when somebody else's constituents are doing poorly, argue that they'll ultimately benefit from the money you give your own supporters.

In truth, with the national debt at unprecedented levels, we ought to be spreading less federal peanut butter around. In any case, Obama's so-called regionalism is a subtle way of redistributing the nation's tax money to urban Democratic constituencies, with far more disturbing implications for personal and political freedom than the War on Poverty ever had.

Obama can afford to antagonize small-town and rural voters because he isn't going to win much support from them anyway. The real challenge for him is getting a political boost from voters in the suburbs, even as he sets his sights on their wallets and lays his plans for undermining their way of life. Obama's utopian hopes require not just income redistribution but government control of how and where Americans live. Yet this president seeks the votes of the very suburbanites whose lives he would upend.

QUIET REGIONALISM

Obama has stocked his administration with proregionalist policy makers. Many of those officials were present at the Brookings conference Obama addressed in July 2009. As noted, the Brookings Institution's Bruce Katz, the regionalist policy wonk who attacked Sarah Palin's supposed "village idiocy," is an administration adviser on these issues. Katz was part of the Obama transition team, so was well placed to fill the government with advocates of "metropolitanism."[23] Obama invoked Katz in his 2008 address to the U.S. Conference of Mayors, and the administration has continued to receive advice from Katz since then.[24]

Although the Obama-Katz-Brookings connection is clear, the role of Myron Orfield, a far more controversial leader of the regionalist movement, is less well known. Now a University of Minnesota law professor, Orfield was a Minnesota state legislator and leader of the drive to force redistributive regional tax base "sharing"—really tax base taking—on Minnesota's suburbs. Orfield has worked closely with Obama's community organizing colleagues at the Gamaliel Foundation and Building One

America for years. He was also a featured speaker at Building One America's White House conference.[25] On top of his close relationship with Building One America, Orfield has been advising the Obama administration for some time.[26] Katz himself cooperates with Orfield.[27] But whereas Katz's residence at Brookings allows him to serve as the moderate face of the movement, Orfield's radical connections and plans are potentially far more controversial.[28]

We'll be learning more about Orfield's controversial tax base "sharing" ideas and his partnership with Kruglik's Building One America below. It's worth noting here, however, that through his work with the White House, Orfield had an important hand in shaping President Obama's global climate change initiative (also known as the Waxman-Markey Bill, or "cap and trade").[29] Few people realize that a bill famous for limiting greenhouse gas emissions—and raising energy costs for consumers in the process—is also an important component of Obama's regionalist playbook. That's because Obama's regionalist initiatives characteristically do not announce themselves as such, but are buried instead inside of other policies and provisions.

In an April 2010 speech, Orfield explained the strategy.[30] First, craft bills, like Waxman-Markey, that funnel federal grants through regionwide metropolitan planning organizations, rather than states or localities. This tends to increase the power of regional governance at the expense of localities—especially suburbs, Orfield's real target. Then use the "accountability provisions" built into bills like the president's climate change initiative and the stimulus package to force regionalist goals—like fighting suburban "sprawl," pressing for the "economic integration" of housing, and the equalization of city and suburban school funding—on localities. In other words, fund localities only through regional bodies, then cut off the grant money unless states and suburbs jump on the regionalist policy bandwagon. As we'll see in chapter 7, the Obama administration has used similar techniques to usurp local control of the school curriculum and is currently positioned to press for de facto mergers of urban and suburban school districts via the same strategy.

The stimulus bill passed, so its "accountability provisions" are available for continued manipulation by Orfield and his regionalist colleagues. Obama's climate change initiative failed to clear Congress, but could easily come back in regulatory form in a second Obama term, or be reintroduced to a more politically sympathetic Congress. The important point is that regionalist plans can be carried out quietly via almost any big bill by making grants conditional on the fulfillment of Obama's regionalist goals.

FROM PEANUT BUTTER TO WATERMELON

The centerpiece of the Obama administration's regionalist policy to date has been the Sustainable Communities Initiative.[31] That program doles out federal money to develop plans for transportation, housing, and land use, but only on condition that the plans are regional in scope and managed by regional governing bodies. Many metropolitan areas have boards or authorities dedicated to specific purposes, like managing a regional transportation network. Some regional planning commissions also offer advice on broader issues of transportation or land use, with local governments' retaining the ultimate right to formulate policy on such issues. The goal of regionalists is to grant these currently merely advisory metropolitan planning boards the power to override the decisions of local suburban governments—with the specific purpose of forcing economic redistribution throughout a given region. The ultimate aim is to use these newly empowered metropolitan supergovernments to impose regional tax base sharing on the suburbs.

So how does Obama's metropolitan policy forward these redistributive goals? Most of the administration's talk about regionalism focuses on economic competitiveness and environmental concerns. The only reason President Obama gave to back up his early public comments about the end of sprawl was the need for "energy efficiency."[32] Yet beneath the administration's preoccupation with green concerns like "sustainability," the redistributive impulse lurks. If you apply for grants under Obama's Sustainable Communities Initiative, for example, you'll find that points are heavily awarded for proposals that advance "regional equity."

Although the Obama administration's Sustainable Communities Initiative is fairly new, we do have one particularly detailed report on its grant program, a 2011 article on a $2 million federal grant to the Capital Area Regional Planning Commission of Madison, Wisconsin, and Dane County. The grant was to develop a regional master plan for transportation and land use. The report is authored by University of Wisconsin law professor Lisa Alexander, a strong supporter of the regional equity movement.[33]

Alexander notes that the Madison area regional planning commission got the grant, in part, by promising to include organizations that "[advance] the interests of traditionally marginalized groups" and by creating a "social equity committee" that will meet and "strategize about how to advance regional equity." Alexander approvingly adds that one partner in the grant is involved in "a grassroots effort with other progressive organizations" and is therefore "ideologically aligned" with "the interests of low-income and underserved populations in the Dane County area." Indeed, a distinctive feature of the Obama administration's Sustainable Communities Initiative is the effort it makes to insert leftist community organizations into regional planning—a position urged on the administration by Kruglik's Building One America.[34]

What's interesting is that despite the lure of $2 million in federal money, several Dane County municipalities pointedly chose not to participate in the "regional planning consortium." Since the board's recommendations will be strictly advisory, Alexander worries that its plans for the redistribution of regional resources will not be enforceable on those municipalities. The point of the Sustainable Communities Initiative is to use the carrot of federal money to lure reluctant suburbs into these redistributive regional schemes. Yet Alexander suggests that it will take coercive state-level mandates, or other forms of compulsion, to make certain the wealth gets spread.

Washington is perfectly capable of applying that kind of regulatory muscle, although the Obama administration is not about to make that move in the run-up to the president's reelection campaign. Consider that in January 1998, halfway through President Clinton's second term, the Environmental Protection Agency threatened to withhold federal transportation funds from the Atlanta region, which had fallen short of federal air-quality standards, unless the state of Georgia agreed to dramatically alter its transportation and land use policies in such a way as to conform to the antisuburban "Smart Growth" agenda. Georgia knuckled under, but only until the end of Clinton's term.[35]

Once "equity plans" have been generated by Obama-funded regional boards across the country (and once the president has been safely reelected), federal regulatory coercion could easily force these plans on reluctant states and suburbs. That is precisely what Obama's friends at Building One America are pushing for.

Hundreds of regional planning grants have been issued under the Sustainable Communities Initiative since 2009.[36] The newly elected Republican House managed to shut off funding for still more grants in 2012, but Obama plans to restore the money in 2013 by taking it out of open-ended HUD monies.[37] Obama's allies at Building One America are pressing him to make nearly all future federal grants for any purpose conditional on state and local adherence to equity plans developed under the Sustainable Communities Initiative—plans that would be heavily shaped by input from leftist community organizations such as Building One America and allied groups. This would effectively turn a modest program for regional planning grants into a lever for radical social transformation.[38]

In time, you can bet that these "equity plans" will begin to include regional tax base sharing. What Obama's friends in Building One America are up to is organizing local political coalitions designed to coordinate with the federal government in a kind of pincer movement to force regional equity plans and tax base sharing on states and suburbs. Yet the American public has barely an inkling of how much the Obama administration has been doing to forward the plan.

For some time, social critic Peter Wood has highlighted the sustainability movement's anti-free-market agenda.[39] Conservative writer James Delingpole has also argued that the "sustainability" movement is a lot like a watermelon: green on the outside and red on the inside.[40] The Obama administration's Sustainable Communities Initiative proves the point. Obama's talk is all green, but the hidden bottom line is juicy redistributive leftism.

OBAMA'S MONEY TRAIL?

We know the Obama administration has sought to provide leftist community organizations with significant influence over the regional planning grants funded by the Sustainable Communities Initiative. Yet Building One America wants more. Not content to have itself and allied organizations assigned a place at the table as various regional equity plans take shape, Kruglik's group is looking for a source of federal funding not controlled by the main recipients of the grant. That is, Building One America wants to have its cake and eat it too. It aims to be a key official player in drawing up federally funded regional equity plans under the Sustainable Communities Initiative while also remaining free to run Alinskyite pressure campaigns against other members of the regional planning bodies it sits on. An independent stream of money, not controlled by the other participants in the federal grant, would allow for that. There are clear signs that President Obama aims to make Building One America's wish come true.

Building One America lays out its detailed funding strategy in a May 2010 report whose key points were forwarded by Mike Kruglik to Shelly Poticha, director of HUD's Office of Sustainable Housing and Communities in March 2010. The report was drawn up by David Rusk, a founding thinker of the regionalist movement and longtime "strategic partner" to both the Gamaliel Foundation and Building One America.[41]

Rusk argues that funding for "grassroots organizing and advocacy groups" under the Sustainable Communities Initiative should not be controlled by the regional bodies that are the official recipients of the planning grants. That's because Rusk wants community organizations like Building One America to serve as "watchbirds" over the governmental recipients of the grant. That is, Rusk wants his Alinskyite organizing buddies to be able to run protests and other pressure tactics against the metropolitan planning organizations and other regional governing consortia that officially receive the federal planning grants.

To achieve this, Rusk suggests either a separate stream of federal funding going directly to regionalist advocacy groups or various schemes for funneling federal money to community organizations indirectly, through the medium of philanthropic foundations. Rusk proposes, for example, that the federal government might channel grants through philanthropic foundations that the Sustainable Communities Initiative would recruit or that federal grants might be offered as matching funds to independently made philanthropic "advocacy" grants.

What Rusk doesn't add, but what anyone who has followed the history of federal grants to the controversial community group ACORN will instantly recognize, is that these indirect funding methods would help to insulate the Obama administration from accusations of direct financial support for his controversial community organizing cronies.

We know that the July 2011 White House Forum on the suburbs sponsored by Kruglik's Building One America was followed by a meeting in the White House wardroom between Kruglik, his lead organizers, and a group of left-leaning philanthropic funders. We also know that just after this meeting, Kruglik was called to meet with Obama in the Oval Office. During that Oval Office meeting, Kruglik let the president know which funders and organizers were present. Afterward, Kruglik's second in command, Building One America Strategic Director Paul Scully, let key funders and organizers know that the Obama administration was aware of their presence at the meeting and supported their efforts.[42]

A reasonable interpretation of this, given all we know, is that in mid-2011 Kruglik was assembling private philanthropic partners to put in place precisely the sort of indirect federal funding mechanisms described in Building One America's 2010 report and letter to the Obama administration. It seems equally likely that President Obama was personally apprised of this funding plan by Kruglik during their meeting in the Oval Office and that Obama was effectively sending a signal of his approval to the philanthropic funders through Kruglik and his deputy, Scully.

This is not to say that there is anything illegal about the funding scheme in question. There is good reason to believe, however, that Kruglik and Obama may be attempting to minimize the potential for explosive public controversy by making the route from federal grant to Building One America's coffers as indirect as legitimately possible. We already know that, for years, ACORN deliberately crafted its own indirect funding schemes to disguise its extensive financial relationship with the federal government.[43] Given the potential controversy of Building One America's antisuburban plans and its historical ties to Obama, substantial insulation looks like a smart move in this case as well, even if it never quite reaches the legally questionable extremes explored by ACORN.

SHAKING UP SUBURBIA

The regionalist program for gradually doing in the suburbs has three main components: 1) Redistribute suburban money to the cities. 2) Force middle-class suburbanites back to the city. 3) Force the urban poor out into the suburbs. The Obama administration has already launched an ambitious initiative to press this last goal of "economic integration" on the suburbs.

While regionalists would like to see the same legal and moral sanctions now applied to racial segregation deployed to force "economic integration" as well, our legal system recognizes no such equivalence. So regionalist Plan B is to shoehorn attempts at economic integration into initiatives ostensibly targeted against illegal racial discrimination. That is exactly what is happening in the Obama administration's important yet little-known battle against New York State's suburban Westchester County—a confrontation the administration itself promises to expand nationwide in the not too distant future.

Although Westchester County has the fourth most racially diverse population in the State of New York, although its housing practices have been praised by previous Democratic and Republican administrations alike, and although studies show that

Weschester's housing patterns are driven by economics, not race, a local civil rights group sued, claiming that Westchester had falsely claimed a commitment to "affirmatively further" federal fair housing goals while applying for a government grant.[44]

Not wanting to risk losing its federal funding, and believing it would get a reasonable settlement from the Obama administration, Democrat-run Westchester invited the feds to intervene and craft a compromise. Bad mistake. Obama's officials used the opening to draw up what looks like a convoluted and excessive settlement, but is in fact precisely designed to force "economic integration" on this suburb, in a case ostensibly about race. The administration now plans to replicate the Westchester settlement in communities across the country.

The initial Obama administration settlement required Westchester to spend $51 million to build 750 subsidized housing units. Of these, 630 must be placed in municipalities with less than 3 percent African American and less than 7 percent Hispanic residents. Knowing that minorities might be reluctant to move to predominantly white districts, the administration required Westchester to conduct affirmative marketing efforts for the new housing. Clearly, this is social engineering, not a genuine effort to halt discrimination.

That financial shakedown was only the beginning. Sensing an opportunity to impose its ambitious regionalist agenda on a timid Democratic-controlled county board, Obama's department of Housing and Urban Development intervened to expand the government's demands—effectively acknowledging that it was now gunning for something much bigger than the settlement of a supposed discrimination case.

Now the Obama administration insisted on gutting Westchester's zoning power—a prime goal. Regionalists have long seen ending a suburb's power to control its own zoning as the way to force "economic integration" on unwilling municipalities.

Obama's HUD then insisted that Westchester County pass "source of income" legislation, although Congress has already rejected such efforts, as has New York State. The change would overturn the long-standing provision of federal law that allows private landlords to choose not to accept tenants whose "source of income" is a voucher from the Department of Housing and Urban Development. In other words, HUD would force private landlords to accept public housing tenants, a very direct path to "economic integration."

Then the Obama administration handed over control of Westchester's housing to an attorney in partnership with a local university, removing local officials from control of their own government's housing policies indefinitely. All this when there had never really been discrimination in the first place, just a clever lawsuit and a county afraid to risk its federal grants or offend a president of the same party.

Here we have a prototype for gutting suburban government and handing it over to regional authorities instead. The Obama administration certainly means to treat it that way. Ron Sims, deputy HUD secretary at the time the expanded demands were first made, said of the new agreement: "We're clearly messaging other jurisdictions across the country that there has been a significant change in the Department of Housing and Urban Development." Then, in October 2011, HUD Assistant Secretary John Trasvina pointedly noted that the administration was "actively investigating" about twenty communities nationwide for Westchester-like treatment. Suburban Marin County, California, is next in line. The Obama administration is clearly promising a major ramp-up of coercive regionalist engineering in a second term.

Despite its national implications, the Westchester case is not well known, with fewer still recognizing its connection to the administration's regionalist goals. Yet in "Shaking Up Suburbia," the liberal *American Prospect* made the point, tying the West-chester settlement to the regionalist commitments of the Obama administration, and especially of HUD Secretary Donovan.[45] The *Prospect* also stressed that the aggressive and sophisticated regionalism displayed by the Obama administration in the West-chester case goes far beyond anything tried by the Clinton ad-ministration.

REGIONALIST HERO

Deputy HUD Secretary Ron Sims, who leveled the first public threat to replicate the Westchester settlement nationally, stepped down from his post in late July of 2011. Until then, Sims had served as the key liaison between the Obama administration and Building One America. Sims gave a major address at BOA's founding conference and has spoken before the New Jersey BOA affiliate.[46] One of Building One America's think-tank arms, the Poverty and Race Research Action Council, early on established a close relationship with Sims and his staffers, and with many other officials and staffers at HUD, and in the Obama adminis-tration as a whole. In meetings and memos, this arm of Building One America has pressed Sims and HUD since the beginning of the Obama administration to take precisely the sorts of steps we saw in Westchester County.[47]

As the three-term executive of Washington State's liberal King County prior to his time at HUD, the charismatic and person-able Sims was one of the most important proregionalist politi-cians in the country. Sims's tenure as the leader of King County is a case study in the sort of public official the Obama administra-tion is looking for.

Determined to force suburban residents back toward urban

areas, Sims created an urban growth boundary with restrictions requiring rural landowners to keep up to 65 percent of their land undeveloped.[48] That law sparked a bitter rural backlash. "Something has gone awry in King County," wrote the *Seattle Times* in 2005. "Across farmland and along country roads, a seething anger is spreading." That rural rage was largely aimed at Sims as protesters caravanned into Seattle carrying signs like RON SIMS, KISS MY GRASS. Sims's growth boundary sparked talk of separating an independent rural county from King.[49]

No wonder. Under Sims's restrictions, country folk had to pay for permits even to take out nuisance vegetation on their own land. Those who had hoped to fund their retirement on the sale of their own land were left with nothing.[50] When Building One America's New Jersey affiliate had Sims in for a talk, it bragged that he had put a stop to suburban sprawl by keeping "96 percent of new construction . . . concentrated in urban areas with only 4 percent in rural areas."[51] A Sims opponent on the King County Council lamented that Sims's land use policies had "essentially created two classes of citizens: those who live inside the urban growth boundary and those who live outside."[52]

Sims's repeated attempts to force high concentrations of low-income housing into King County suburbs also led to extended battles. While Sims's heavily subsidized low-income housing developments have garnered praise from fellow regionalists, it's hard not to wonder if they had anything to do with the King County budget crisis Sims left behind when he departed for Washington, D.C.[53]

In any case, although Executive Sims did not seek out a federal job, his regionalist policies obviously spoke for themselves. He was phoned "out of the blue" by the Obama transition team and offered the number two slot at HUD.[54]

WAR AGAINST SUBURBIA

Although the president has worked to downplay the goals and even the existence of his urban-metropolitan policy, one bold critic has highlighted his real intent. Joel Kotkin, an urban expert of moderate-conservative bent, argued powerfully in January 2010 that the Obama administration had in effect launched a "war against suburbia."[55] In Kotkin's words, "for the first time in memory, the suburbs are under a conscious and sustained attack from Washington." He went on to cite the antisuburban regionalist ideology guiding many Obama appointees. He also pointed to Obama administration plans to steer up to 90 percent of all future development into what are already the densest urban neighborhoods. This would be accomplished not only through draconian regulatory controls on suburban and exurban development but also through tolls on the interstate highway system and fees that would require many Americans to pay to park in front of their own homes. Over the long term, said Kotkin, Obama aims to force suburban and exurban Americans back to city centers, cramming the country's population into a series of new, hyperdense Manhattan-style downtowns.

Writing shortly after Scott Brown's upset victory in the Massachusetts special election to determine Ted Kennedy's successor in the U.S. Senate and Republican victories in off-year elections in New Jersey and Virginia, Kotkin argued that these Republican wins were powered by the same middle-income suburban swing voters who had earlier put congressional Democrats and President Obama into power. These middle-class suburbanites sensed that Obama's policies held little advantage for them, said Kotkin, even if the regionalist thinking behind the president's moves had never been fully laid out.

Kotkin cited plenty of evidence to show that Americans very much continue to prefer the privacy, quiet, safety, and good schools available in the suburbs. He also punctured simplistic contrasts between supposedly alienated and isolated suburbanites and happily communal city dwellers. Kotkin showed that minorities—African Americans, Latinos, and Asians—now make up more than 27 percent of the suburbs, ratifying the area's appeal and giving the lie to outdated stereotypes of white flight. Kotkin also did a great deal to cast doubt on the assumption that suburban living is ecologically harmful. The dispersion of work centers to the suburbs, for example, now actually means shorter commute times in the suburbs than the city. Meanwhile the rise of telecommuting is likely to make continued dispersion environmentally feasible for years.

According to Kotkin, Obama's "war against suburbia reflects a radical new vision of American life," a vision designed to "replace a political economy based on individual aspiration and association in small communities, with a more highly organized, bureaucratic, and hierarchical form of social organization." Although Kotkin is absolutely right about this, his sweeping critique of the Obama administration's urbanism has never caught on. Instead Kotkin has been something of a voice crying in the wilderness. Why?

For one thing, President Obama's refusal either to highlight or even to spell out the real goals of his urban-metropolitan policy has helped prevent it from becoming a target. And while administration officials have indicated their intention to enact the kind of draconian land use regulations and onerous driving and parking fees Kotkin cited, those moves are far too controversial to get through Congress. They'll have to be directly or indirectly imposed through regulation instead. These are initiatives for the president's second term should he have one.

Kotkin's writings are suffused not only with warnings to the

Obama administration about the political peril of taking on middle-income suburban swing voters but also with a sense of puzzlement that Obama would flirt so seriously with antisuburban regionalism. In contrast with the Clintons, who "expressed empathy with suburban and small-town voters," says Kotkin, "the Obama administration seems almost willfully city-centric."[56] In his view, "this is an overt stance that neither Bill nor Hillary Clinton would likely have countenanced."[57] (President Clinton did offer some support to the antisprawl movement toward the end of his term.) Especially given the thinness of the ecological case against suburbia, Kotkin asks, why pick a fight with the nation's most powerful swing constituency?

OBAMA'S PAST IS PRESENT

What Kotkin doesn't see is that Obama's oldest and deepest political convictions are at work here. Kotkin briefly cited the influence on the Democratic Party of what he calls "an elaborate coalition of new urbanist and environmental groups."[58] Yet he never explores the precise nature of that "new urbanist" coalition or its links with Obama's past. Since Obama hasn't been especially forthcoming about any of this, why should Kotkin or anyone else notice?

The hard-left regionalism that Obama drank in from his community organizing colleagues in the Gamaliel Foundation blames "flight" to the suburbs by middle-class whites and minorities alike for the poverty of the cities. Obama's leftist community organizing colleagues have struck up an informal alliance with environmentalists, whom they use as a shield to disguise their radical plans for income redistribution in the form of regional tax base sharing. And through Building One America, Obama and his community organizing mentors have a long-term strategy for overcoming the political perils of their regionalist stance. Yet the groundwork must first be laid, and the president's reelection secured. Only in a second term can the truly serious risks can be taken. Precisely because Obama's regionalism does indeed reveal him to be to the left of the Clintons, it needs to be kept under wraps for now.

Interviewed in 2008 in *Governing* magazine, Obama's metropolitan guru Bruce Katz said that it would take five years to "embed" a full-fledged proregionalist apparatus in the bureaucracy of a friendly administration.[59] Funny how that works out to one year into a second Obama term.

Obama's current urban-metropolitan policies having been explored, it is time to turn in earnest to the deepest layer of his antisuburban plans. To do this, we need to explore the history of the Gamaliel Foundation and its offspring, Building One America. So let us investigate the world of Obama's radical community organizing mentors and their place in the national campaign to abolish America's suburbs, a campaign now being quietly but actively sponsored by the president of the United States.

CHAPTER THREE

IN UP TO HIS EYEBALLS

"We are battling apartheid in America." So said Obama's onetime organizing mentor Mike Kruglik in 2005, explaining the philosophy behind his crusade for regional equity.[1] At the time, Kruglik was directing the regionalist efforts of the Gamaliel Foundation, a national network of community organizations that Obama himself had helped launch in the mid-1980s. Today Kruglik leads the Gamaliel offshoot Building One America, which fights for regionalism in partnership with the Obama White House, although few Americans have any idea that this is the case.

AN ORGANIZER AT HEART

Comparing this country's patchwork of urban and suburban governments with South Africa's viciously oppressive apartheid system is an extremist notion and a view none too friendly to the United States. Yet Kruglik's claim to be battling "American apartheid" is not an isolated growl from a radical in a moment of rhetorical flamboyance. Rather, equating America's pattern of local government with South Africa's historic system of institutionalized bigotry is the Gamaliel Foundation's core message. Gamaliel's longtime leader and early Obama mentor Greg Galluzzo attributes the creation of America's suburbs to "racism and greed."[2]

We need to learn more about the philosophy and history of the Gamaliel Foundation's regional equity crusade. That's because President Obama has adopted this movement and shaped his administration's policies to its goals. Obama in fact was a charter member and sponsor of Kruglik's regionalist battle. Gamaliel is so central to the regionalist movement that in telling the story of Obama and Gamaliel, we largely describe the story of regionalism itself. Obama's regionalist past opens a window on the president's thinking on urban policy today.

Ultimately that is the point. Because Obama's regionalist commitments have never waned, his history of support for this movement is the best way to make sense of his policies. Obama's radical Alinskyite convictions aren't some long-gone phase. They live on and will profoundly shape America's future should the president secure reelection.

Kruglik himself has said as much. Just a month after Obama was inaugurated, Kruglik spoke about the president to Sean Kirst, a newspaper columnist in Syracuse, New York. Obama "remains an organizer at heart," said Kruglik, and is "focused on confronting the greatest challenge in American history—the long tragedy of separation by despair, by race and class, that plays out in violence, neglect and addiction in our cities."[3] Further summarizing Kruglik's remarks, Kirst explained: "Obama understands that to simply talk about [residential segregation by class and race], even with fierce or inspiring words, will only create more division if he speaks to a nation with no mechanism in place for real change." That mechanism, said Kruglik, could only be created by further organizing at the local level.

So Kruglik is arguing that the commitments of Obama's community organizing days are not a thing of the past, that the president is still strongly focused on the goals of the regional equity movement, and that Obama is reluctant to say as much for fear of creating a political backlash before grassroots organizing efforts like Gamaliel's are more advanced. Could Kruglik merely be interpreting Obama's intentions in light of his own hopes for the regionalist movement? Maybe, but Kruglik's claims tally with Obama's actions (salting regionalist policies and policy makers throughout his administration and quietly collaborating with Kruglik's own Building One America) and with what even sympathetic left-leaning observers call Obama's preference for a stealth urban policy. Kruglik also speaks from a long and close acquaintance with Obama, extending from the president's earliest organizing days in Chicago right through his years in the U.S. Senate and the presidency.

THE RULING CLASSES

The clearest statement of the philosophy behind the Gamaliel Foundation's regional equity crusade can be found in the ambitious ten-year plan, promulgated by the group in 1999, for spreading regionalism across the country.[4] That plan opens with a manifesto describing Gamaliel's efforts as a battle against "American apartheid." The word "apartheid" suggests race as the central issue, but the statement itself has far more to say about conflict by class.

This 1999 manifesto blames America's divisions of race and class on the machinations of the rich, variously identified as "the wealthiest 1 percent," "the richest 20 percent," or "the ruling classes."

Public institutions, we are told by Gamaliel, simply carry out plans engineered by the wealthy ruling classes. The result is a "neocolonial situation," in which reliance on property taxes to support local municipal services helps the rich escape from their responsibility to care for the poor. In opposition to this, the Gamaliel Foundation has helped create "a new kind of people's organization," focusing "unified mass-based agitation" on issues like tax base inequity. "Only through geographically-based organizing at the metropolitan level," we learn, "can enough power be built to transform America." Only that can prevent the wealthy ruling classes from keeping the American people "divided and subjugated."

One of the more interesting themes in the manifesto is the treatment of America's middle class. Ostensibly, Gamaliel's regionalist call to arms is a defense of the country's endangered middle class. Yet the statement reluctantly acknowledges that the rich, who supposedly dominate and rule America, often enjoy "the collaboration and support of the white middle class."

Gamaliel fails to add that the African American middle class is gravitating toward the nation's suburbs and also largely supports our system of local governance. Such an admission of course would undercut Gamaliel's image of an "American apartheid." The suburbs aren't exclusively white. They are multiracial and multicultural.

Ultimately, Gamaliel's leaders care most about class, but pumping up the idea that America is a racist society lends the group an air of moral righteousness and allows it to downplay its more controversial class-based positions.

Gamaliel's manifesto depends on the idea that ordinary people don't understand their own choices and are misled into believing they are better off than they really are. The old-fashioned Marxist term for this is that the masses suffer from "false consciousness" and that the role of the radical vanguard is to disabuse them of their illusions. The Gamaliel Foundation's version of this is that the wily ruling classes have duped America's middle class into believing that the suburbs are the fulfillment of the American dream. Galluzzo himself has elsewhere taken on this supposed delusion:

> Many people think that what drives urban sprawl is that people yearn for the American dream: their own home with its garage and its lawn to mow. In fact much of what drives it is racism and greed.[5]

Galluzzo apparently believes that the ruling classes have kept themselves in power by dangling the false suburban dream in front of the country's middle class, thereby playing upon the racism and greed of ordinary citizens in order to keep the people divided and dominated in "neocolonial" oppression.

It's tough to find any daylight between Gamaliel's proclamation and a flat-out Marxist analysis. For those who suspect that many Alinskyite organizers are thinly disguised socialists, Gamaliel's 1999 regionalist manifesto provides strong evidence. Yet it isn't necessary to buy that particular interpretation of Gamaliel's ideology to grasp the basic point. It seems fair enough to say that Obama's Gamaliel mentors are hard-left radicals who are deeply skeptical about traditional American values, preoccupied with class conflict, and determined to "transform America." Clearly, their goal is also to disabuse the middle class of its supposedly delusional suburban American dream.

OBAMA JOINS UP

The Gamaliel Foundation, established in Chicago in 1968 as a fair housing group, was reorganized by Greg Galluzzo in 1986 into a consulting service for community organizations.[6] Alinskyite groups that sought out Galluzzo for training and advice became part of the Gamaliel network. Galluzzo and his top lieutenants, Mike Kruglik and Jerry Kellman, served as Obama's original organizing mentors, and Obama's Developing Communities Project was one of the first groups to join Galluzzo's network.[7] So Obama was very much in on the founding of Gamaliel in its current form.

In 1980 Galluzzo and his wife, Mary Gonzales, had formed the group called the United Neighborhood Organization (UNO) of Chicago, based in the city's predominantly Hispanic neighborhoods.[8] During his years with UNO, Galluzzo refined Alinsky's techniques of confrontation and disguise into methods later taught by the Gamaliel Foundation. At UNO, for example, Galluzzo often staged showdowns with political figures not to gain decisive victories but to fail spectacularly. Forcing politicians surrounded by rowdy protesters to reject demands for greater government spending generates anger and helps gin up membership. Politicians were physically chased—pursued to their homes or sometimes trapped, as happened, for example, to Republican senator Charles Percy, who was once chased into a women's restroom. Galluzzo, whose politics are far to the left of liberal, shunned labels and presented himself and his organizers as post-ideological "pragmatists." He also focused his organizing efforts on religious congregations, promising to increase attendance at declining urban churches. In the view of many, however, Galluzzo's promise of help was really just a scheme to hijack control from priests and ministers and hand it over to congregants who'd received his community organizer training.

Where was Mike Kruglik in all this? Although Kruglik is the least known of Obama's early organizing mentors, as the director of Building One America he is now a key link between Obama's radical Alinskyite past and his presidential present. Unsurprisingly, as Galluzzo's top lieutenant Kruglik has been at the very center of the Obama-Gamaliel nexus.

Kruglik actually held Obama's first Chicago community organizing job just before Obama himself arrived.[9] The future president was hired to take charge of the Developing Communities Project (DCP), a group based in predominantly African American churches on Chicago's South Side. Kruglik had been assigned to the group, but members asked for an African American organizer instead. Kruglik and his replacement hit it off right away. Obama was famously a workaholic during his early organizing years, but Kruglik, who was now one of Obama's trainers, used to drag him out to blues or jazz clubs or have him come over to watch the Bears, the Bulls, or the White Sox on TV. Obama continued to visit Kruglik when he returned to Chicago on breaks from law school.[10] Kruglik, for his part, remembers Obama as "the best student he ever had . . . the undisputed master of agitation."[11]

After leaving DCP in Obama's hands, Kruglik took charge of his own Chicago-area Gamaliel affiliate, the South Suburban Action Conference (SSAC).[12] In 1992, around the time Obama returned to Chicago after graduating from Harvard Law School, Kruglik made news as the target of a series of protests by disaffected pastors and church members from his group.[13] The protesters called for Kruglik's resignation from the SSAC and carried signs like CROOKED LEADERS CAN'T RUN A STRAIGHT ORGANIZATION.[14] It must have been odd for an Alinskyite organizer accustomed to leading African American pastors and their congregants in protest to be the target of the kind of demonstration he usually fomented.

The pastors said Kruglik had ignored their wishes and concerns. In a press release the protesting ministers alleged that Kruglik had been using their churches "to build power for himself and the Gamaliel Foundation."[15] They charged financial mismanagement as well. Kruglik and his supporters vehemently denied these charges and explained the protests as a vendetta against the firing of a son of one of the dissatisfied pastors.

The rights and wrongs of that firing and the financial accusations may never be resolved. Yet the broader complaints by pastors about Alinskyite organizers' commandeering congregations
for their own political purposes are part of a long trail of similar
accusations. That kind of conflict doesn't discourage a Gamaliel
organizer. The leadership training sessions run by Gamaliel organizers like Galluzzo, Kruglik, and Obama himself are designed
to break down a potential recruit's ego, only to build it up again
around the goal of Alinskyite power seeking. Recruits are taught
that if they really want power (a core Alinskyite goal), they need
to prepare to be disliked and attacked and then to turn the polarization to their own advantage.[16]

LIKE A THUNDERBOLT

But something serious was eating away at Gamaliel's top organizers in the early nineties. The leadership was gripped by a pervasive
sense of failure. Obama had left for law school out of a feeling that
he could do more for Chicago's South Side through politics than
through organizing. Some have cited that move to suggest that
Obama long ago turned his back on community organizing.[17]
Nothing could be further from the truth. Obama retained and
deepened his organizing ties in subsequent years, pouring money
into the coffers of Chicago's most radical Alinskyite groups and
coordinating with them in his legislative battles.

Yet it's true that Obama and his Gamaliel mentors all had the
sense that their efforts to improve the lives of people on Chicago's
South Side had not been working. Said Kruglik of that era: "We
were always asking each other, 'Why do this work that busts your
balls so bad all the time?' "[18] The real problem was that even the
minority of organizing campaigns that actually succeeded in

prying loose extra money from local politicians didn't seem to change anything fundamental about the neighborhood.

This was the concern of Gamaliel's top leaders when, in 1993, a Minnesota state representative named Myron Orfield spoke to the network's Minneapolis affiliate about regionalism.[19] Orfield was the leader of a left-leaning coalition of Minnesota state legislators who'd been fighting for regional tax base sharing.[20] It was an alliance of politicians from cities and less well-off inner-ring suburbs determined to forcibly commandeer tax money from previously independent middle-class suburbs in the greater Minneapolis–St. Paul region. This was a way for cities to get hold of suburban tax revenue without the need for formal annexation.

More broadly, Orfield attributed the problems of urban poverty to the very existence of suburbs. The point hit Gamaliel like a thunderbolt. So that was why even its successful attempts to pry more spending out of politicians weren't working! Government spending alone can't save the cities so long as the suburbs continue to drain the urban tax base. All of a sudden the drive to better yourself through discipline and hard work, the hope of saving enough money to move into your own home, all the elements of the classic American dream came to seem like the source of the American nightmare instead. The hope of moving to a freestanding house, long considered the engine of American prosperity and betterment, came to represent, for Gamaliel's organizers, the ultimate cause of poverty.

In December 1995 Orfield addressed a meeting of Gamaliel's most senior organizers while Galluzzo and Kruglik, now thoroughly convinced by the regionalist gospel, steered the network toward regionalist organizing. Gamaliel struck up a "strategic partnership" with Orfield and two other experts, the former Albuquerque, New Mexico, mayor David Rusk and john powell (powell prefers to spell his name without capital letters), the founder-director of the University of Minnesota's Institute on Race and Poverty.[21] By 1999 regionalism had been well established as Gamaliel's guiding orientation, and the ambitious manifesto and ten-year plan discussed above had been published.

Had Gamaliel's leaders really discovered the hidden cause of urban poverty or merely a way to blame the failures of their big-government schemes on America's suburban middle class? The answer is the latter, I'll argue when we take up the writings of Gamaliel's regionalist advocates in chapter 5. Yet by 1995 Obama's Chicago-based organizing mentors were concentrating their efforts on the regionalist crusade, and they haven't let up until today.

Following up on the 1995 embrace of regionalism as Gamaliel's guiding orientation was the Chicago-based Metropolitan Alliance of Congregations (MAC), an association of 107 area churches "organizing against regional inequities fostered by sprawl," created in 1996.[22] Mary Gonzales, Galluzzo's wife and fellow organizer, served as MAC's founding executive director.[23]

Gonzales is credited by sympathetic chroniclers of the regionalist movement, Manuel Pastor, Jr., Chris Benner, and Martha Matsuoka, with developing a language based on "hope and abundance" rather than "zero-sum" concepts like "scarcity and fear."[24] These same observers attribute Obama's own rhetoric of "hope" to his time with Gamaliel. Commenting on the 2004 keynote address to the Democratic National Convention that rocketed Obama to national fame, Pastor, Benner, and Matsuoka say: ". . . we think we know where [Obama] learned to talk like that: he was a community organizer in Chicago for the Gamaliel Foundation, exactly as the network was trying to lift up regional equity as a new organizing framework, strategy, and language."[25] Actually Obama's time as a salaried organizer had ended a bit before Gamaliel's formal embrace of the regional equity movement. Yet his ties with the group only deepened as its regionalist focus took hold.

Gonzales may have talked a good game of "hope, unity, and abundance," but it's tough to take that line seriously. Polarization was the aim of the tactics that she and Galluzzo perfected in Chicago.[26] Speaking to a sympathetic publication in 1999 about MAC's campaign to force tax sharing on Chicago-area suburbs, Gonzales said, "This is not going to be a consensus-building campaign. I'm not sure we even realize how ugly this could get."[27] A booklet used to train Gamaliel organizers also acknowledges that tax base sharing and other goals of the regionalist movement are seen by many suburbanites, with good reason, as "directly counter to their self-interest."[28] Gamaliel's organizers may lay on a lot of talk about "win-win," "hope," and "abundance," but their redistributive plans are zero sum, and they know it.

FOLLOW THE MONEY

Gamaliel's divisive tactics were on full display in March 1997, when three busloads of MAC protesters chased the Republican Illinois senate president, James "Pate" Philip, after he declined an invitation to attend one of their meetings.[29] The protesters bottled up Philip at his home, where they chanted for him to come out. One of Philip's neighbors, whose driveway was blocked by the protesters, angrily jumped into her car, headed for the protesters' buses, and narrowly averted a collision. Pursuing a legislative "target" to his home was typical Gamaliel fare.

What's more, Barack Obama was financing it. Although he was no longer a salaried Gamaliel organizer, Obama had become the leading force on the board of the Woods Fund of Chicago, pushing to increase the foundation's financial support for community organizing. As an influential board member who was also an Illinois state senator and the pride of the foundation, Obama was able to see to it that his old Gamaliel colleagues received substantial grants. Obama has been a major source of funding for the regional equity movement from the moment of its birth. How has this point been missed?

Let's say you were to get hold of a hard-to-find copy of the Woods Fund of Chicago's "1996 Annual Report." If you were to browse through it, the one thing sure to stand out would be the glowing profile up front of the former Weather Underground radical and Woods grantee Bernardine Dohrn (with photo).[30] At the time, Dohrn was the director of the Children and Family Justice Center at Northwestern University Law School. Bloggers during the 2008 presidential campaign were able to highlight Woods Fund gifts to radical recipients like Dohrn, notorious community organizations like ACORN, and of course Jeremiah Wright's church. With standouts like that, nobody noticed that the Woods Fund listed a forty-thousand-dollar gift in 1996 to MAC.[31] Nor did the special fifteen-thousand-dollar Woods grant that year to Mike Kruglik for a project "to address urban revitalization in a more comprehensive manner" stand out.[32] Although the record clearly establishes that Obama was in on the ground floor of the regional equity movement, nobody's yet realized it.

Woods Fund annual reports and form 990 filings from 1993 through 2002, when Obama served on the board, are chock-full of grants for Gamaliel's regionalist crusade, even if none of that is readily apparent. The Gamaliel network in the Chicago area was a complex collection of groups nested within groups. The Woods Fund commonly sent grants simultaneously to the Gamaliel Foundation itself, to Gamaliel's Chicago-area affiliate MAC, and then to the component organizations of MAC—for example, the Alliance of Congregations Transforming the South Side (ACTS), the Joliet Area Church-based Organized Body (JA-COB), and of course Kruglik's SSAC.[33] There were also grants to Gamaliel affiliates in nearby states.[34] Put them all together, and

close to a quarter of Woods's total grants for community organizing in 1998, for example, went to Gamaliel-affiliated groups,
all of whose campaigns had by this time been largely centered on
regionalism.[35] (Quite possibly the total is higher, since several
other listed groups may have been Gamaliel affiliates.)

This was no case of Obama's merely rubber-stamping recommendations made by staffers or other board members. On the
contrary, during the years he served on the Woods Fund board,
Obama led the faction looking to channel ever more funding to
community organizers. A committee chaired by Obama actually
published a special report in 1995 suggesting ways for the Woods
Fund to increase its support for community organizing.[36]

This was the precise moment when Gamaliel was moving toward its formal embrace of regionalism, and Mary Gonzales was
a member of the committee advising Obama on that report.[37]
The list of community organizers Obama consulted while drawing up his study includes Greg Galluzzo, Mike Kruglik, and numerous others from the Gamaliel network.[38] In short, from the
moment Gamaliel's regionalist crusade began, Obama did everything in his power to expand the Woods Fund's financial support
for those efforts.

Obama's commitment to funding community organizing was
sincere but hardly disinterested. Once he became an Illinois state
senator in 1997, Obama set about coordinating legislative campaigns with his Woods Fund–supported Alinskyite allies. There
was even a theory about it, a conscious effort to create a good
cop/bad cop dichotomy. The idea was for community organizers
to angrily confront targeted politicians while allowing liberal legislators and policy experts to remain on friendly terms with their
opponents. A description of the strategy, published in the Woods
Fund's "2001 Annual Report," was written by Joshua Hoyt, an
organizer who had once worked under Galluzzo and Gonzales at
UNO of Chicago.[39]

So Obama, who was the main backer of grants for community organizing at the Woods Fund, knew perfectly well that his old colleagues were using his financial awards to stage Alinsky-style confrontations with his political enemies. Of course it was important that as the legislative good cop in a good cop/bad cop game, Obama not place himself on the scene during these demonstrations. Yet the 1995 Woods Fund report on community organizing that Obama personally supervised actually bragged about coaxing money from donors reluctant to abet "confrontational tactics against the business and government 'establishments.'" Obama not only approved of these Alinsky-style attacks on local political leaders but was leading the charge to support them with foundation cash.[40]

Obama was clearly running this good cop/bad cop strategy on Pate Philip, the leader of the Republican majority in the Illinois senate. After all, he was financially supporting the organizers who chased down Philip. And this was totally consistent with the confrontational goals outlined in Obama's 1995 report on support for community organizing. The attempt to trap Philip in his own home, run by Obama's close colleagues and well reported in Chicago, could not have been a mystery to Obama, who kept the money flowing year after year to the very activists who went after his legislative foe. So while Obama developed a reputation for dealing politely and fairly with his GOP colleagues, he was funding his radical Gamaliel allies to chase down the Republican leader at his home.

Did Obama actively meet and coordinate with MAC and Gamaliel on their regionalist campaigns? We know for certain that this happened in 2004, when Obama spoke at a MAC rally as he was running for the U.S. Senate.[41] We also know that Obama worked closely with Mike Kruglik to advance Gamaliel's regionalist goals when he served as a U.S. senator. Kruglik's son actually joined Obama's U.S. Senate staff.[42] A 2007 MacArthur Foundation report on the regionalist movement notes: "It is almost unheard of for a U.S. Senator to attend a public meeting of a community organization, but Senator Obama attended a Gamaliel affiliate public meeting in Chicago."[43] As a U.S. senator Obama also went to the congressional leadership and demanded that a Gamaliel-backed provision be inserted in a transportation bill, citing his special relationship with the group.[44]

That is what we know for sure, but there's also evidence that Obama's cooperative relationship with Gamaliel's regionalist campaigns extends back to the very beginning of his political career. MAC held a couple of major regionalist rallies in Obama's home district of Hyde Park, one in 1996, just as Obama was about to take his seat in the state capital, and one a couple of years later.[45] Reports list senior politicians present, but don't bother to name the state senators attending those rallies. In all likelihood, Obama has been closely collaborating on regionalist campaigns with his Gamaliel allies from his very first days in elected office. At any rate, we know that Obama was actually funding Gamaliel all that time and that he has worked to advance Gamaliel's regionalist policy proposals from his U.S. Senate days right through to his presidency.

AN OPTIMAL LEVEL OF FOG

We've learned that the ideology and tactics of Gamaliel's regionalist crusade are radical and that Obama has been in with this group up to his eyeballs for decades. Yet there's more to the story of Gamaliel and regionalism than that. In a sense, Gamaliel's history traces the shifting fortunes of the broader national movement against sprawl.

There was a lot of debate about the alleged problem of suburban sprawl in the latter half of the 1990s, just when Gamaliel's regionalist crusade was in high gear. *Time* magazine's 1999 cover story, "The Brawl over Sprawl," signaled the rise of the issue to national prominence.[46] For the past decade or so, however, the sprawl controversy has been much less prominent, although it has resurfaced from time to time. Something intervened to lower the volume of the debate over sprawl, and the fate of Gamaliel's regionalist crusade helps explain how things got dialed down.

Few Americans have even heard of regionalism, much less regional equity organizing. Pastor, Benner, and Matsuoka, who chronicle and support the regional equity movement, grant that it's been flying "under the media radar screen."[47] Debates over suburban sprawl, on the other hand, are more familiar, as are "green" efforts to discourage driving. Pastor, Benner, and Matsuoka suggest that the motives of the antisprawl crusade have been left "deliberately fuzzy," to create what they call an "optimal level of fog."[48] That fog, they say, keeps attention on well-publicized arguments about economic competitiveness and the environment while obscuring the redistributionist goals that motivate the movement's core. This strategy, they add, "amounts to a sort of 'stealth equity.' "[49]

Myron Orfield's plan to allow cities and a few declining inner-ring suburbs to raid the tax money of other suburbs has everything to do with that stealth. It was Orfield who convinced Gamaliel to embrace the regionalist cause, and Gamaliel has long served as a national mouthpiece for Orfield's redistributive plans. Yet the controversy over regional tax base sharing (not really "sharing" because it's forced), is exactly what the antisprawl movement is reluctant to pull out of the fog.

A 1997 report in *Crain's Chicago Business* said Chicago civic planners discuss tax sharing schemes, "only in hushed tones."[50] "Doesn't it sound a bit like communism?" *Crain's* asked. *Crain's* is clearly raising the specter of communism half-jokingly—but only half. Scott Bollens, a professor of planning at the University of California, Irvine, makes a similar point in an article entitled "In Through the Back Door: Social Equity and Regional Governance."[51] Bollens calls social equity a "third-rail issue."[52] Political leaders, he says, address questions of redistribution only indirectly, "through the back door," via laws and administrative directives imposed by the federal government, like pollution limits.[53] Bollens suggests that these less than frank rationales make it easier to gain political support for redistributive moves.[54] Gamaliel, however, takes the opposite route, agitating for explicitly redistributionist policies, tax base sharing above all.

By embracing the regional equity crusade, in fact, Gamaliel has become a bit less circumspect than most Alinskyite groups about its own leftist goals. Robert Kleidman, a sociologist from Cleveland State University, has studied Gamaliel's regionalism for years. He notes a bit skeptically that Gamaliel organizers formally "retain Alinsky's claim of being non-ideological."[55] Yet Kleidman also argues that Gamaliel's advocacy of openly redistributive goals like tax base sharing has forced its ideology closer to the surface.

And what is that ideology? Kleidman doesn't directly say, but he notes that "progressive" organizers run the gamut between left-liberal and socialist, and he highlights the socialist origins of the regionalist perspective.[56] Kleidman strongly advocates even greater ideological openness from groups like Gamaliel. He means this in a friendly way. He now organizes for Mike Kruglik's Building One America and was present at BOA's White House conference and the later debriefings.[57]

BACKFIRE

Orfield's controversial plans to forcibly reduce fiscal disparities between suburbs and cities created trouble for Gamaliel from the very start of its regionalist campaign. That big Hyde Park rally in

October 1996 (which Obama surely helped fund and was likely present at as well) featured numerous allusions to Orfield's recently released MacArthur Foundation–funded study of Greater Chicago.[58]

Yet Orfield's study ran into immediate trouble, even from friends of regionalism. The MacArthur Foundation was extremely uncomfortable with Orfield's suggested political program: having cities and inner-ring suburbs gang up on the bulk of the suburbs to force them into tax base sharing. It reportedly declined to publish Orfield's political recommendations. It also appeared to delay publication of Orfield's study and asked that he not advocate any particular policy solution when presenting his analytical findings at MacArthur-sponsored events.[59] An influential Chicago attorney on MacArthur's board, who was also broadly sympathetic to Gamaliel and regionalism, expressed real concerns about Orfield's political approach, warning that it could easily lead to class "warfare."[60] So while Gamaliel's regionalist crusade was far more openly redistributionist than most antisprawl efforts, the frankness created a backfire.

The following year, 1997, Gamaliel ran a regionalist campaign in St. Louis through an affiliate called Metropolitan Congregations United (MCU).[61] This time tax-based revenue sharing was passed over as too controversial. The battle was constructed instead around the issue of sprawl. MCU began working with two sympathetic state legislators to draft a bill that would enforce an urban growth boundary, thereby forcing new development back toward the city. There was also an attempt to block the construction of added freeway lanes between St. Louis and nearby St. Charles County. No sense making it easier for people to drive home to the suburbs.

The result was a deeply divisive battle that quickly alienated even those state legislators who had tried to help Gamaliel and MCU. The *St. Louis Post-Dispatch*, initially sympathetic to the protesters, started having second thoughts when Gamaliel's campaign got going.[62]

At the beginning of MCU's so-called smart growth campaign, the mayor of St. Louis, Clarence Harmon, struck up an alliance with Gamaliel and virtually went to war against several local suburbs. Mayor Harmon made news when he claimed that the cost to the region of building new water lines and other infrastructure for the growing suburb of St. Peters would be an astronomical thirty-seven thousand dollars for each new home. Challenged on the accuracy of his figures, the mayor couldn't say where he'd got them.[63] (They probably came from Gamaliel, whose Chicago allies floated similar figures, while admitting they couldn't be validated.[64]) The *Post-Dispatch* sharply took the mayor to task for pulling wild numbers out of a hat.[65] Goaded on by the protesters from Gamaliel, hypercontentious legislative hearings soon followed, leaving local and state leaders calling for a deescalation of the increasingly ugly confrontations between city and suburb.[66] Yet Gamaliel was elated by the conflict because it held out the promise of exactly the sort of polarized legislative battle over suburbia it'd been trying to provoke all along.[67]

What happened next is remarkable. Businesses and politicians in Greater St. Louis tried to settle the conflict by proposing a major program of financial assistance to the city. That might sound like victory for Obama's community organizing allies, but Gamaliel actually took this offer of funding for the city as a defeat.[68] That's because Gamaliel really does buy the arguments of regionalists who say that the battle between cities and suburbs is a zero-sum game. It's not enough, in the eyes of regional equity organizers, for government or business to offer financial aid to reconstruct the cities. For Gamaliel activists, even a traditional big-spending War on Poverty is only the beginning. Regional equity organizers really believe that the very existence of suburbs, with their own independent tax bases, dooms cities to disastrous decay. That's why this movement is truly radical. A bit of financial assistance isn't enough. Only massive structural change will do. Formally or informally, further suburban expansion will have to be blocked, and the suburbs will need to be effectively abolished and their taxes shifted toward the city if Obama's old organizing buddies are to be satisfied.

So even without foregrounding the controversial tax sharing proposal, the radicalism of the regionalist agenda ended up alienating Gamaliel's allies in the state legislature, who recommended backing off the growth boundary idea in the short term. Gamaliel St. Louis was forced to retreat on the issue and repositioned itself for a lengthy and incremental campaign instead.[69]

Something quite similar happened to Gamaliel's regionalist campaign in Northwest Indiana, which ran parallel to the ones in Chicago and St. Louis in 1996 and 1997.[70] Gamaliel's prestigious experts, Orfield, Rusk, and powell, were invited in to speak to its affiliate, the Northwest Indiana Federation of Interfaith Organizations (one of the groups Obama was supporting through the Woods Fund).[71] The local papers were rhapsodic in praise at first. But everything changed when the *Hammond Times* got a good look at Gamaliel's proposals. Its banner headline was ECO-NOMICS OF ENVY. In an editorial, the paper called Gamaliel's program "a document dripping with unconcealed hostility toward the south part of the county. . . . It is not so much a plan for equitable development as a declaration of war. . . . The unabashed aim is to stop the wheels of progress in south county and to force them to come to the north."[72] In the end Gamaliel's Northwest Indiana affiliate realized that it would have to pull in its horns and battle on more modestly over a longer period.[73]

Gamaliel fought high-profile regionalist battles throughout the late 1990s, just as the sprawl issue was breaking through in the country at large. Yet again and again Gamaliel discovered that Americans largely reject the goals of the regionalist movement, at least when those goals are presented straightforwardly. Gamaliel's move toward a longer, low-profile, more incremental battle almost certainly has a lot to do with the general decline of sprawl as a national controversy over the last decade or so.

PRESIDENT GAMALIEL

Yet Gamaliel could hardly have anticipated that one of its own would someday become president of the United States. That unanticipated good fortune meant that Gamaliel leaders like Kruglik and "strategic partners" like Orfield would morph into government advisers in the service of a chief executive who was himself an old Gamaliel hand. It meant the spread of regionalist policies and policy makers to every part of the administration. It meant that a grassroots regionalist movement could now depend on systematic support from the president of the United States. It all culminated in the creation of Building One America, the Gamaliel offshoot led by Kruglik. By shedding the Gamaliel name, the group serves to minimize its ties to Obama's controversial past and now prepares the way for a bold new strategy to transform the very structure of American life.

In a sense, Building One America simply transplants Gamaliel's regionalist campaigns to the White House. Paul Scully, who serves just beneath Kruglik as the group's lead organizer, ran Gamaliel's Northwest Indiana regionalist campaign in 1996 and 1997 and was listed as a consultant to Obama's Woods Fund report of 1995.[74] As noted, Obama's Woods Fund helped pay for Scully's original Northwest Indiana campaign. Kruglik and Scully also trained campaign workers at Camp Obama in 2008.[75]

Obama's Alinskyite organizer past truly lives on in the present. An October 2011 meeting of the BOA affiliate Building One Pennsylvania in Lancaster had been billed as nonpartisan yet left invited GOP lawmakers none too happy when an address by HUD Secretary Shaun Donovan turned the event into a virtual Obama campaign rally. What's more, the organizers tried to pin down elected officials to quick yes or no answers of support or opposition, a patented Gamaliel technique designed to produce either capitulation or polarization. Republican state senator Lloyd Smucker, who wouldn't play along, left the rally fuming after he was prevented from getting out his points. A local newspaper columnist condemned the event's partisanship, and an angry letter to the editor claimed that one Republican state senator in particular had been badly mistreated.[76] We could write it all off as a misunderstanding or mistake were it not for the fact that Gamaliel's polarizing techniques regularly produce such results and in fact are designed to do so.

Obama's own time with Gamaliel generated similar incidents. When young Obama led his group, the Developing Communities Project, in a campaign to have asbestos removed from a local public housing project, for example, the effort culminated in a meeting at which Chicago Housing Authority Director Zirl Smith was supposedly invited to give his side of the story. Yet the meeting ended abruptly when Smith was angrily chased from the scene by members of Obama's group after the hapless fellow was refused a microphone for trying to say more than yes or no.[77]

As for policy, the New Jersey Regional Coalition, a Gamaliel affiliate and now the core component of Building One America, pushed for regional tax base sharing in the New Jersey legislature in 2006.[78] So there's much continuity in the program of Obama's regionalist allies, although less expectation now of a quick victory.

In another sense, however, a great deal has changed. Robert Kleidman, who wrote that article pushing Gamaliel toward even greater ideological openness, is now starting a Building One America affiliate in Ohio. Kleidman recruited a group of local Ohio officials to attend BOA's White House forum. What makes

Building One America different from Gamaliel is that its base consists primarily of local elected officials, rather than clergy or lay leaders in congregations.[79]

Why the change? The discouraging lesson Gamaliel was forced to take from the early failures of its regionalist campaign was that it would have to slow down and work incrementally. Yet the more aggressive takeaway was the need to create a base of supporters in state legislatures before running divisive campaigns for regional tax base sharing and urban growth boundaries. Now Building One America can work to assemble legislative coalitions for regionalism's polarizing agenda, using the prestige and resources of the president of the United States. Kruglik himself has said that Obama cannot openly carry the regionalist message to the country until a mechanism for "real change" is in place. Building One America is that mechanism. If safely reelected, Obama would use Building One America to assemble proregionalist legislative coalitions in the states and only then offer public support for regionalism's high-conflict agenda.

In a quiet way the process has already begun. Whereas Bollens reported that overtly redistributive policies are seldom discussed by regional officials, we saw in chapter 2 that Obama's Sustainable Communities Initiative essentially forces regional planning bodies to develop regional equity plans. Those plans could focus Alinskyite agitation by Gamaliel and Building One America in a second Obama term. Kruglik and Gamaliel/BOA strategic partner David Rusk have actually been advising the Obama administration on how to include equity provisions in the Sustainable Communities program for some time.[80]

Yet whether you favor or oppose urban growth boundaries and bold plans for tax base redistribution, shouldn't the country have an opportunity to debate this transformative agenda before Obama secures reelection? The president has been none too eager to place the regionalist program on the table for public discussion, although as we'll see in chapter 5, it is arguably his most cherished hope. Obama hasn't leveled with the American people on this critical and controversial part of his agenda, and that is just plain wrong.

The president's relative silence on regionalism is also strongly reminiscent of the stealthy incrementalism of Saul Alinsky, the founder of community organizing and the idol of Obama's regionalist mentors. Obama's continuing participation in the very same Alinskyite movement that focused his early political career establishes clear continuity between the president's radical past and his administration today. It also reopens the question of just who Saul Alinsky was and what the organizing technique he created has to do with the conduct of his most famous acolyte, Barack Obama. We turn to that question in the following chapter.

CHAPTER FOUR

SAUL ALINSKY RADICAL

The Republican presidential candidate Newt Gingrich got it right when he described Barack Obama during a Republican debate just before the 2012 South Carolina primary as a "Saul Alinsky radical."[1] When Gingrich followed his South Carolina win by repeatedly highlighting Obama's Alinskyite background in a victory speech carried by every major television network in the country, the mainstream press was forced to break with its usual practice of ignoring the president's radical past.[2] There followed a minifirestorm of one-sided pieces slamming Gingrich and downplaying Obama's Alinsky connection, a difficult task given that Obama is both a longtime admirer of the founder of community organizing and an accomplished practitioner of Alinsky's methods.

It would be tough to find a more egregious example of bias than the mainstream press's reaction to Newt Gingrich's comments on Obama's Alinsky connection. After his victory in the 2012 South Carolina Republican presidential primary, Gingrich said, "The centerpiece of this campaign, I believe, is American exceptionalism versus the radicalism of Saul Alinsky."[3] "Saul Alinsky radicalism is at the heart of Obama," Gingrich added in an interview with CNN.[4] The press, if it were doing its job, should then have explored the issue by examining the influence of Alinsky on Obama and by interviewing experts who both favored and opposed Obama. Serious media would have communicated the views of those who thought the Alinsky-Obama connection was highly significant and those who thought it was exaggerated, then let readers, viewers, and listeners decide for themselves. Nothing of the sort happened.

You couldn't tell articles in the mainstream press from opinion pieces on the left. Headlines screamed the bias, calling Alinsky Gingrich's bogeyman and asking why Gingrich was so "obsessed" with the founder of community organizing.[5] Remember, Obama used to teach Alinsky's principles to community organizers and himself proudly touted the formative influence of his community organizing days when he announced his candidacy for president. Yet the press granted Gingrich's point no credence, nor were any but Gingrich-hostile experts interviewed.

Because the press has been of no help, we're going to have to take up the issue ourselves. That's because Obama's Alinskyite background is much more than a campaign "gotcha"; it is a profound window into the president's goals and tactics. Obama's continuing support for Mike Kruglik's crusade to abolish the suburbs shows that the president's Alinskyite past never really passed at all. The mainstream press's refusal to report on Obama's radical ties has kept the public in the dark about the Alinskyite aspects of his policies in the present and ill prepared for his even more Alinskyite plans for the future.

OBAMA IN ALINSKY'S WORLD

What exactly do we mean when we say that something is Alinskyite, that it is inspired by the ideas and techniques laid down by Saul Alinsky, the founder of community organizing? Who was Saul Alinsky and what did he believe? This question has everything to do with how President Obama acts in the present and what he plans for the future. We've seen that President Obama has thrown his administration's support behind his Alinskyite allies' audacious project to abolish the suburbs. To grasp the philosophy and strategy behind that project, we need to school ourselves in the Alinsky way.

The truth about Saul Alinsky is difficult to come by. Trickster that he was, Alinsky knew how to mask his intentions. His opponents stumbled by throwing imprecise charges of communism, which Alinsky was clever enough to sidestep. The master's artful dodging has served as an object lesson for his followers ever since.

Obama lived at the center of Alinsky's legacy. An organizer's organizer, Obama was arguably the most important financial supporter of the Alinskyite enterprise in Chicago from the mid-1990s through the early 2000s. In 1995 he chaired a major push to increase funding for community organizing in the city and nationally. Obama worked at the confluence of a troika of left-leaning foundations that supported Alinsky's followers, sitting on the boards of two of them, the Woods Fund of Chicago and the Joyce Foundation. Obama's own community organizing had been supported by the third member of the trio, the Wieboldt Foundation.[6]

The leaders of these three foundations, of which Obama was one, revered Saul Alinsky and had a deep understanding of his life and work. Just before Obama ascended to the highest ranks of this philanthropic world, all three foundations helped fund the research behind Sanford Horwitt's definitive Alinsky biography, and Obama surely knew Horwitt's work.[7] Read the broader literature on community organizing, which Obama devoured voraciously, and you will understand who Alinsky really was. Yet the truth is rarely placed before the public in unvarnished form.

Here I am going to connect the dots on Alinsky's story more explicitly than anyone to my knowledge has previously done. Yet everything I show is familiar, in its essence, to knowledgeable organizers, of whom Obama was certainly one. Finding out who Alinsky was is important because it shows us the man who inspired Obama in Chicago and whose political lessons the president absorbed. More important, Alinsky's ideas and techniques continue to inform the work of Mike Kruglik and his group, Building One America, and the president, who backs their movement.

Alinsky's ideological reticence, his pragmatic gradualism in the service of hard-left goals, and his intentionally polarizing confrontation tactics have profoundly shaped both President Obama and the regionalist crusade he supports. It helps to see the model that knowledgeable community organizers like Kruglik and Obama have in mind when they employ these tactics today.

In sum, we need to cut through the carefully controlled public portrait that the media have accepted uncritically from Alinsky's close supporters and amplified to America at large. Alinsky, the founder of community organizing, is President Obama's Moses, and Obama is Alinsky's Joshua. Who is Alinsky, really; how has he influenced Obama; and how have the media suppressed that connection?

THE REAL SAUL ALINSKY

Saul Alinsky was not a member of the Communist Party. He had reasons for that, but dislike of communism wasn't one of them. Alinsky's originality was figuring out how to be a hard-leftist without either joining an extremist party or touting an explicit ideology. Alinsky called himself a pragmatic radical.[8]

Alinsky's technique was to advance a far-left agenda piece by piece, without announcing a larger goal or providing an ideological justification. He led his groups unofficially, from behind. He was puppet master, not field commander. Alinsky's ideal was to promote an ideological agenda without seeming to be an ideologue or even to have an agenda. Calling himself a pragmatist was a way both to describe and to disguise this new form of leftism.

Alinsky strongly sympathized with the Communist Party. He supported it without ever joining up. Alinsky's creative leaps were variations on organizing techniques he learned from Chicago's Communists. Community organizers don't advertise this history, but they do know it. In the words of Robert Kleidman, a lead organizer of Building One America, who was present at the White House forum on the suburbs, "Saul Alinsky developed his style of organizing in the 1930s, influenced by the Congress of Industrial Organizations and the Unemployed Councils of the Communist Party."[9]

In the era of Obama the mainstream press is eager to soft-pedal the truth about Alinsky's radicalism and to redefine him as a colorful but benign social reformer. That picture is profoundly misleading.

COMMUNIST ORIGINS

Chicago was a major organizing center for America's Communist Party during the 1920s and 1930s.[10] In the twenties the city's Communists, guided by Marx's precept that workers would lead the revolution, focused on labor organizing. Workers, however, showed little interest, and the party made no significant headway until the Great Depression raised the possibility of stirring up unrest among the unemployed. Because the unemployed did not go to work, the best way to organize them was by neighborhood.

Chicago soon became a center of a new neighborhood-based form of organizing, the Communist-led Unemployed Councils, which were the first radical community organizations in the modern sense.[11]

Chicago's Communists first tried to push the city's unemployed toward violent revolution. When it turned out the workers were more interested in getting jobs than in overthrowing the government, real community organizing was born. A fascinating memoir, *Steve Nelson: American Radical*, tells the story of the first party member to take charge of citywide organizing for the Unemployed Councils.[12] Nelson and his comrades spent their first few weeks with the Unemployed Councils "agitating against capitalism and talking about the need for socialism."[13] They soon realized how little they had to offer even sympathetic listeners.

What people really wanted to know was how to pay the rent, buy food, and just survive until the glorious Communist Revolution arrived. Nelson explained: "It was from involvement in the daily struggles that we learned to shift away from a narrow, dogmatic approach to what might be called a grievance approach to organizing. . . . We spent much of our time simply learning the welfare rules in order to be effective. We couldn't just give speeches about the downfall of capitalism. . . ."[14] So neighborhood organizing taught Chicago's Communists to downplay ideology and focus instead on a program of concrete demands. The hope was that winning small reforms would rally the public to the Communist banner over time, after which the party would mobilize the masses and lead them to overthrow capitalism.

But even these scaled-back revolutionary plans proved difficult to realize. By the mid-thirties, except for certain predominantly black areas of South Chicago where unemployment remained very high, Communist Party organizers had begun to shift away from the Unemployed Councils, pouring instead into unions affiliated with the Congress of Industrial Organizations (CIO).[15]

Out of this mix of Unemployed Councils and Communist-dominated CIO unions on Chicago's South Side, Alinsky was able to create something new.

Alinsky once bragged that the Communist Party saw his first community organization, the Back of the Yards Neighborhood Council, as the ideal united front.[16] By "united front" or "popular front," the Communists meant groups that they quietly controlled, even if the membership included many non-Communists. Alinsky's first community organization was one of those Communist-front groups, but his later community organizations were not. They did, however, stick with the organizing principle of the original united front. Alinskyite groups assemble people from a variety of political orientations but are steered from behind by hard-left (although not literally Communist) organizers.

Alinsky stayed out of the Communist Party for two reasons. First, the Communists' slavish obedience to Moscow and their insistence on strict ideological discipline were poor fits for his ornery, independent personality.[17] Second, he realized that the label was heavy baggage. He could go farther, faster without it. Yet Alinsky was what used to be called a fellow traveler, a strong sympathizer with the Communist Party's long-term socialist goals and an admiring student of its militant tactics.[18] Alinsky's friend Leon Despres, himself a member of the Socialist Party and not on good terms with the Communists in the 1930s, said of Alinsky: "I don't think he ever remotely thought of joining the Communist Party [but] emotionally he aligned very strongly with it."[19]

The politics of Saul Alinsky and his community organizations are notoriously hard to pin down. According to his biographer Sanford Horwitt, "Throughout Alinsky's life there was confusion about where to place him and his concepts on the political spectrum. . . ."[20] One of Alinsky's techniques of disguise was to confess everything but in a fashion that simply confused people by fragmenting the truth and dissolving the context. In a well-known *Harper's Magazine* interview in 1965, Alinsky mentioned his work during the thirties raising money for the Abraham Lincoln Brigade (American volunteers who fought against Franco's Fascist forces during the Spanish Civil War), raising money for sharecroppers down south, and helping stop the evictions of city people who couldn't pay rent.[21] Thirty years after the fact, few would have recognized Alinsky's account for what it was: a confession of heavy involvement in the central organizing projects of the Communist Party of the thirties. The truth is fragmented here, and the context dissolved.

Another favorite technique of ideological disguise was what Alinsky's biographer calls "innocence by association"—for example, pointing to support from clergymen, supposed arbiters of good judgment. Left unsaid was that many of these clergy were hard-leftists themselves.[22] Alinsky also liked to reference America's founders. "You should never have an ideology more specific than that of the founding fathers," said Alinsky, who then intoned, "for the general welfare."[23] By picking out the most collectivist phrase he could find from the Preamble to the Constitution, Alinsky managed at a stroke to deny being ideological at all and to identify his pragmatism with a vaguely socialist-sounding slogan bearing the imprimatur of the Founding Fathers. The Alinskyite recipe for public relations: fleeting and indecipherable confessions covered by a veil of supposed pragmatism, all wrapped up in a red, white, and blue package.

FRONT GROUP

Alinsky's first community organization, the Back of the Yards Neighborhood Council, centered on the residential neighborhood next to Chicago's meatpacking industry. Alinsky was drawn into it by a prominent Communist organizer, Vicky Starr.[24] In 1939 Starr was trying to help the Packing House Workers Organizing Committee (PWOC), the CIO-backed union still struggling for company recognition, to build community support. Alinsky himself later described the PWOC as a Communist-dominated union.[25] PWOC had been a small, peripheral labor group until the merger of several rival unions under CIO sponsorship put it in the driver's seat.[26] Seizing an opportunity to control a union at the heart of a major national industry, the Communist Party "mobilized its entire Chicago apparatus behind the drive in the stockyards . . . [d]irecting its neighborhood units to make organization of the packing industry their first priority."[27]

In setting up his first community organization—with the goal of gaining official recognition for the PWOC—Alinsky worked closely with Herb March, the head of the Communist Party in Back of the Yards, a charismatic leader of the Back of the Yards PWOC union local, a hardened veteran of the Unemployed Councils, and a public member of the American Communist Party's Central Committee.[28] Alinsky's biographer Horwitt tells us that "Alinsky was broadly sympathetic with March's politics."[29]

As very public Communists, Starr and March would never have been able to garner support for a Communist-dominated union from local Catholic clergy. With no formal party affiliation, however, Alinsky was able to bring the clergy in.[30] He recruited a group of young, left-leaning Catholic priests to his cause while convincing more traditional priests that cooperating with the union would allow the church to "beat the Communists at their own game."[31] As Alinsky summarized his feat in an interview with *Playboy*, "To fuck your enemies, you've first got to seduce your allies."[32] So the very first Alinskyite community organization was a Communist-front group, built on Alinsky's successful deceptions. Controversial figures like Vicky Starr and Herb March were able to fade into the background while their ace community organizer conned neighborhood priests into dropping their opposition to a Communist-dominated union.

Since the leadership of PWOC included many veteran Communist Party organizers from the days of the Unemployed Councils, the union carried on its battles using direct action protests commanded not from the union's head office but by party organizers and grassroots leaders on the shop floor.[33] A favored tactic was "rizz-ma-tizz," an action set off when a union steward walked through his department with his arms folded across his chest or his hat cocked to one side. At a signal, workers would move frantically to look as if they were producing at breakneck speed when in fact they were cutting back.[34] Alinsky's devilishly mocking and confrontational direct action tactics are turbocharged versions of rizz-ma-tizz. When Alinskyite organizers paralyze a bank by filling its lines with people trying to change pennies into dollars, the tactical similarity is obvious.

Another example illustrates the continuity of tactics from the days of the Unemployed Councils through the meatpacking struggle and through Alinsky's own innovations. Back in the early thirties Unemployed Council members would surround welfare offices, refusing to let government workers leave until their demands were met. Sometimes trapped government clerks would faint or just leave work and never return.[35] Alinsky's friend and compatriot Herb March applied this tactic to the packinghouse.[36] Workers would trap managers in their offices at the end of the day and keep them from leaving for home until all union grievances were satisfactorily settled. These thug tactics inspired Alinsky's own techniques of going directly to the homes of "targets" and intimidating family members and neighbors in an effort to break resistance to demands.

STILL SOCIALIST

It is sometimes claimed that Alinsky abandoned his socialist sympathies after the thirties, accepting the parameters of America's capitalist system and agreeing to work within them.[37] This view cannot stand up to a reading of his 1945 book *Reveille for Radicals* or his later public interviews.[38] It's clear from his 1972 *Playboy* interview, for example, that Alinsky shared the New Left's goal of destroying capitalism. He advocated nonviolent incrementalism not on principle but because he believed it to be more likely to work.

It's also tough to read the second chapter of *Reveille for Radicals* without coming away convinced that Alinsky was a socialist. Here he explained what authentic radicals should desire: "Radicals want to advance from the jungle of laissez-faire capitalism to a world worthy of the name of human civilization. They hope for a future where the means of economic production will be owned by all of the people instead of a comparative handful."[39]

Alinsky supported the central Marxist tenet of public ownership of the means of production. His biographer Sanford Horwitt suggests that Alinsky's preferred political position, for all its ambiguity, might best be defined as "democratic socialism."[40] Horwitt adds that "in spite of his apparent sympathy for an unspecified American brand of socialism, Alinsky positioned himself above the familiar ideological battles."[41] An "apparent" socialist sympathizer who publicly positioned himself above the ideological fray, Alinsky offered a model of ambiguity for other radicals eager to navigate around America's dislike of extremists.

Robert Fisher, a prominent historian of community organizing, offers the following critique of Alinsky: "Organizing projects such as those of Saul Alinsky, which completely deny the leadership role of the organizer and emphasize letting the people decide, are often either dishonest or manipulative, or parochial and undirected. . . . Organizers bring an ideology, skills, experience, and perspective to their work; they owe it to neighborhood people to share this with them openly and honestly. Not to do so will in the long run increase suspicion."[42]

Fisher, not a conservative critic but himself a leftist organizer, is effectively confirming Alinsky's ideological stealth as well as the tendency of supposedly democratic "people's organizations" to serve as fronts for the manipulation of leftist organizers.

PURE ALINSKY

Establishing that Barack Obama has been profoundly influenced by the thought and practice of Saul Alinsky is a bit like proving that beaches are sandy. It would appear to be undeniable, though many in the media have risen to the challenge. Because Obama's long-standing ties to Alinskyite radicalism have the power to do him political harm, little effort has been spared by his partisans to minimize the connection.

Let us remember that it was Barack Obama himself who first identified his personal and political odyssey with Alinskyite community organizing. The famous photo of Obama teaching an organizing workshop by diagramming Alinsky's power concepts on a blackboard was initially posted on Obama's own campaign Web site.[43] Obama highlighted the formative effect of community organizing on his political identity from the moment he announced his presidential campaign.[44] Indeed, when he first ran for public office in 1995, he explained that he hoped to be a new kind of politician-organizer.[45] After he was elected to the U.S. Senate, Michelle Obama told a reporter, "Barack is not a politician first and foremost. He's a community activist exploring the viability of politics to make change."[46] Until the public learned more about what Alinskyite organizing actually entailed, Obama was eager to brag about the connection.

According to the Obama biographer David Mendell, "Alinsky's life mission and his methodologies are both central to Obama's modern political message."[47] The Obama biographer Edward McClelland calls Obama's famous asbestos battle, from his early organizing days, "pure Alinsky."[48] Obama's original organizing mentors from that time, Jerry Kellman, Mike Kruglik, and Greg Galluzzo, were close followers of Alinsky's.[49] Kellman studied directly with Alinsky.[50] Galluzzo, who moved to Chicago hoping to meet Alinsky just before he died, never met the man, yet considers himself "as St. Paul who never met Jesus." Galluzzo, in other words, regards himself as Alinsky's "best disciple."[51] As we've seen, Galluzzo, Kruglik, and Kellman all were leading organizers at the Gamaliel Foundation, the grassroots muscle behind the regionalist crusade.

Obama has ties to Alinsky through several other chains of influence. He worked closely with the very radical Midwest Academy, whose founder, Heather Booth, studied under Alinsky in the same cohort as Jerry Kellman.[52] Obama also received training from the Industrial Areas Foundation, the organizer training institute founded by Alinsky.[53] And despite his denials, Obama has extensive ties to the notorious community group ACORN, which was very much shaped by Alinsky's thought.[54] Obama taught seminars for ACORN on "power," so the famous photo of Obama diagramming Alinsky's ideas could easily have come from one of his training sessions for ACORN. Ideologically, a great many of Obama's organizing mentors and colleagues shared Alinsky's socialist sympathies.[55]

Yet Obama and his fellow organizers weren't slavish followers of the founder. If there was one area where Obama and his partners at ACORN and the Midwest Academy broke with Alinsky, it was the relationship between community organizing and electoral politics. Obama and his fellow organizers swept aside Alinsky's aversion to electioneering and forged alliances between political officeholders and community organizers, often openly supporting political candidates.[56] Obama, a pioneer of this new approach, saw himself as a politician who worked and thought like an organizer. The partnership of Mike Kruglik's Building One America and the Obama administration is the ultimate example of this post-Alinsky turn by organizers to close alliances with politicians.

ALINSKY AND REGIONALISM

The significance of the post-Alinsky shift in community organizing should not be exaggerated, however. Alinsky died well before the modern regionalist movement came into being, yet it is no coincidence that his most loyal followers now serve as grassroots leaders of the antisuburban crusade. What is it about regionalism that connects to the legacy of Saul Alinsky?

Alinsky liked to work quietly, and focusing on the local level helped him do that. Yes, he sometimes staged high-profile confrontations designed to make news and intimidate "targets" or "enemies" into submission. Yet he also took advantage of the fact that local politics in America frequently plays out beneath the media radar screen. It's tough to organize a national political crusade for hard-left goals while a more easily assembled local campaign to pressure obscure city and county officials has a good chance to work and without stirring up undue attention or opposition.

Alinskyites pride themselves on finding unexpected ways to pressure politicos by researching obscure statutes and bureaucratic practices that nobody pays much attention to. This is especially easy to do on the local level. Organizing cities and a few relatively impoverished inner-ring suburbs also makes it possible to create a movement without even attempting to recruit more conservative rural and suburban voters.

In short, Alinsky liked to work not from the top down but from the ground up, and his followers still draw on that insight. Starting locally gave Alinsky stealth when he wanted it and extracted maximum leverage from minimal organizational effort. It also allowed an American hard left to flourish in cities, where a rump remained, even as the rest of the country rejected the politics of class warfare and redistribution. The limitation here is the need for patience. But if you are willing to wait, to build a political movement bit by bit, then the Alinsky method is for you.

Regionalism was a perfect fit for Alinsky's followers—Obama's mentors—because it had the potential to transform America into a redistributionist nation, yet in a way that could be done piece by piece, starting at the local level. That avoided the flak that openly proposed federal redistributive programs would immediately elicit at the national level and allowed organizers to maximize their leverage in the localities where they were already strongest.

As president, of course, Obama is perfectly positioned for "top down" rather than "bottom up" politics. Yet the truth is, Obama is still an Alinskyite at heart. He would rather move slowly, from the ground up, toward his most controversial redistributionist changes, so as to minimize public opposition. He can do that by partnering with his Alinskyite colleagues and lending quiet support to their locally focused crusades. Obama can promulgate regionalist regulations without major publicity, and he can send administration officials out to meet with Alinskyite groups without much notice from the national media. He can also salt his administration with regionalist advisers, with few in the media even recognizing that it's happening, much less grasping what it means.

What, then, is Obama's debt to Alinsky? It chiefly consists of four things: pragmatism, stealth, left radicalism, and confrontation. Obama's regionalist crusade embodies pragmatism, stealth, and left radicalism. And the president's regionalist Alinskyite colleagues are already practicing confrontation at the local level, even as they reap administration support. Expect Building One America's confrontational tactics to escalate in a second Obama term.

BOGUS DEFENSE

While the president's Alinskyite legacy certainly includes support for his old colleagues in Building One America, it also extends well beyond this. Like Alinsky, Obama styles himself a pragmatist on a wide range of issues. That accurately describes the president's patient incrementalism yet disguises his sweepingly redistributionist goals—that is, his stealth leftism. What about confrontation?

The president's supporters sometimes say that despite his admiration for the founder of community organizing, Obama himself shunned Alinsky's use of confrontation tactics. The Obama campaign's Attack Watch Web site hit back at Gingrich by making the same point: Obama didn't go in for Alinskyite hardball.[57] That is wrong. Obama did participate in Alinsky-style confrontations during his early organizing years, although knowledge of this has been suppressed by his allies.[58] For example, Obama helped plan and execute a demonstration that broke in on a private meeting, after which the targets—James Fitch, the president of South Chicago Savings Bank, and local community leaders— were surrounded and effectively intimidated.[59] The group was trying to come to an agreement to allow local landfill expansion in return for Waste Management Corporation spending millions of dollars on job training, scholarships, housing, health care, and day care in the community.[60]

Obama also papers over his aggressive Alinskyite tactics in *Dreams from My Father.* The famous mass meeting over asbestos staged by Obama, for example, was not the accidental fiasco he portrays it as but a product of his mentor Greg Galluzzo's intentionally polarizing tactics.[61] Above all, Obama funded his community organizing mentors for years from his position on the boards of various Chicago foundations, knowing full well that the beneficiaries of these grants were eager to stage confrontations.[62] It's true, however, that Obama prefers to play the good cop in a good cop/bad cop game he stages with his Alinskyite organizing partners.[63] I lay out the hidden story of Obama's radical organizing days and his ties to Chicago's highly confrontational Alinskyite left in my political biography of the president, *Radical-in-Chief.* There I also follow the Alinskyite trail through to the Obama presidency.

WAR ON FOX NEWS

President Obama's attempts to stoke political polarization and intimidate enemies through aggressive targeting are easy enough to spot. The failed 2009 "war on Fox News" is an example.[64] The Obama administration's battle against Fox had all the earmarks of a classic Alinskyite confrontation. Even mainstream outlets called it a White House war against Fox, and Obama-friendly commentators said that the White House had foolishly gone beyond subtle favoritism for sympathetic news outlets to treating Fox as "an outright enemy."[65] Of course singling out targets or enemies and attacking them in intrusive and highly public ways in order to intimidate opposition and gin up your own followers are exactly what Alinsky recommended.

Obama's war on Fox News began when the White House chief of staff Rahm Emanuel and the White House political guru David Axelrod hit the airwaves in October 2009 to declare that Fox was not a legitimate news organization. Flummoxed by media interest in unflattering stories about the notorious Obama-allied community group ACORN and the radical Obama aide Van Jones that only Fox had been willing to cover, the White House tried to delegitimize the network. The goal was to prevent other news organizations from picking up on Fox's stories. As this was going on, Obama personally gave vent to his anger against the network in a private meeting with friendly media. In an NBC interview he also effectively supported and echoed his lieutenants' attacks on Fox.

When the administration tried to cut Fox News out of a standard pool interview with the White House executive pay czar Kenneth R. Feinberg, other press organizations rebelled and refused to let the network be excluded. Documents obtained in 2011 through a Freedom of Information Act request by the public interest group Judicial Watch reveal that despite repeated administration denials, it did in fact intentionally attempt to exclude Fox from a pool interview with one of its officials.[66]

While the backlash by news organizations and commentators forced the administration to retreat from its public war against Fox, the incident is revealing. Resistance from mainstream outlets and a wide swath of opinion leaders shows just how extreme and confrontational the administration's instincts are and how little it values the existence of a traditional marketplace of ideas. In a profound sense, Obama's war on Fox was illiberal, a product of Alinskyite radicalism rather than traditional Democratic Party politics. And Obama would have stuck with the battle had his own supporters not rebelled.

Calling on Hispanics to "punish your enemies," as Obama did at the height of the 2010 midterm election, is classic Alinskyite language.[67] Obama's repeated attacks on the Chamber of Commerce during the 2010 election were efforts to jump-start a populist, antibusiness movement of the left, a long-held dream of Obama's Alinskyite organizing colleagues. It failed at the time, but Obama succeeded later when his attempts to stir up class warfare by slamming "millionaires and billionaires" in their "corporate jets" helped inspire Occupy Wall Street.[68]

Obama's support for his mentor Mike Kruglik's campaign to abolish the suburbs makes it clear that the president's Alinskyite past has never disappeared. Kruglik was an original trainer of Obama, and Kruglik's new group, Building One America, is a continuation, under another name, of the Gamaliel Foundation's regionalist crusade. Obama himself once taught Alinsky's ideas and techniques to fledgling Gamaliel organizers. Greg Galluzzo, Gamaliel's longtime leader and one of Alinsky's top disciples, has trained members of the New Jersey Regional Coalition, the core of Kruglik's new group.[69] From his position on the board of the Woods Fund of Chicago, Obama secured funding for his Alinskyite colleagues' regionalist crusade from its very beginnings in the mid-1990s.

BUILDING ALINSKYITE AMERICA

Today, support for the president's Alinskyite mentors' sweepingly ambitious organizing efforts is White House policy. We've seen evidence from Pennsylvania that Alinsky-inspired confrontation tactics have been used in the new White House-supported regionalist crusade. Recall that an October 2011 meeting of the Building One America affiliate Building One Pennsylvania ended in angry recriminations from Republicans who attended what had been billed as a nonpartisan meeting. The affair turned into a de facto Obama campaign rally, and legislators were forced into yes or no answers by the same pinning technique taught by Obama's Alinskyite mentor Greg Galluzzo. State senator Lloyd Smucker, who refused to play along with the yes or no game, was prevented from putting his case to the meeting, infuriating his supporters.[70] Under Galluzzo's tutelage, Obama created a similar scene at an asbestos meeting during his organizing days in Chicago.[71] And remember, that decidedly Alinskyite affair in Pennsylvania was ostentatiously supported by Obama's HUD secretary, Shaun Donovan, who bragged to the crowd that we now had a community organizer in the White House.

Certainly the redistributionist ambitions at the core of the regionalist movement are consistent with Alinsky's socialist sympathies. As for Alinskyite stealth, Obama has played it brilliantly, keeping the very existence of his heavily redistributionist plans well under the public radar, even as he's put large portions of his antisuburban scheme into place. He has been orchestrating his regionalist coup behind the scenes in classic Alinsky fashion. And if a program designed to effectively abolish America's suburbs isn't radical, what is?

While liberal journalists and friendly biographers have in the past acknowledged the influence of Alinsky's thought on the president, Obama's community organizing has been downplayed by both the president and his supporters of late. Especially since conservatives found out what Alinskyite influence really meant, Obama's radical past has become a political liability. While Obama's newfound reticence about his Alinskyite background and sympathies is a transparent evasion, those in the press who understand his game are happy to play along.

The left-leaning biographer Sasha Abramsky, very friendly to Obama, has noticed the pattern of press avoidance: "Much of the media, including his biographers, have concluded that the community organizing period of Obama's life should be accorded relatively little space, assuming those years simply reflected the radical foibles of a young man trying to find himself. What these commentators missed was that the beliefs that led Obama into community organizing a quarter century ago, along with the skills he perfected while an organizer, were both key to who he became politically. . . ."[72]

Contrary to Abramsky, the media avoid Obama's early radicalism not because they think it's irrelevant but because they recognize that drawing the connection too tightly, even when done by a sympathetic biographer like Abramsky, is politically harmful to the president.

LAUGHABLE BIAS

In light of all that we've learned, let us now have a look at the many attacks on Newt Gingrich's remarks highlighting the president's Alinskyite background after the 2012 South Carolina Republican primary. The most commonly made point in both left-wing opinion pieces and mainstream articles was that Obama had never met Alinsky, who died when Obama was a mere child in Hawaii.[73] That's like saying you can't be a Marxist if you never met Marx. Obama's own organizing mentor Greg Galluzzo never met Alinsky yet considers himself Alinsky's foremost disciple. Galluzzo trained Obama, and Obama taught Alinsky to Galluzzo's junior organizers. Now Obama carries on Galluzzo's crusade against the suburbs, a crusade Obama supported financially from its very first moments. Obama never met Alinsky, but then Lenin never met Marx.

Other stories called the Obama-Alinsky link tenuous or emphasized that to the extent it existed it had been important only early in Obama's career.[74] None of that is true. From his position on the boards of several Chicago foundations, Obama was the most important financial supporter of Alinskyite organizing in

Chicago during his time in the Illinois senate. Not only did he fund highly confrontational Alinskyite groups like ACORN, the Midwest Academy, and the Gamaliel Foundation, but he successfully led efforts to increase foundation spending on these and other community organizations.[75] And as we've seen throughout this book, Obama has maintained a close political alliance with his Alinskyite mentors from his earliest organizing days right through to his presidency.

Writing in the *New Republic*, the leftist historian Michael Kazin deployed two of Alinsky's own defensive techniques, "innocence by association" (the Catholic connection) and resort to the Founding Fathers.[76] But many of Alinsky's Catholic supporters were hard-leftists themselves, and support for Alinskyite organizing, particularly the recent grants to ACORN, remains deeply controversial within the American Catholic Church.[77] As for the founders, Alinsky was clever enough to turn them into leftists via selective quotation.

The most extraordinary response of all came from Alinsky's premier biographer, Sanford Horwitt. Widely quoted making light of Gingrich's warnings, Horwitt told Lynn Sweet of the *Chicago Sun-Times*, "Alinsky was emphatically not a Marxist, he was not a Communist ever."[78] Yet in his biography Horwitt suggests that Alinsky's preferred political system might be "democratic socialism." He also speaks of Alinsky's "apparent sympathy for an unspecified American brand of socialism." It was Horwitt who approvingly quoted Leon Despres affirming that Alinsky "emotionally aligned very strongly" with the Communist Party. Then there are Alinsky's own words from *Reveille for Radicals*, quoted earlier, in which he yearns for a world in which "the means of economic production will be owned by all of the people instead of a comparative handful."

It's certainly possible to argue about what Alinsky's ideology actually was. Yet by Horwitt's own account, simply saying that

Alinsky was not a Marxist or Communist is far too simple. Imagine what would have happened, however, if Horwitt had said to Sweet, "Well, Alinsky never joined the Communist Party, and he wasn't a slavish follower of Marxist ideology; but he was probably some sort of democratic socialist, and in practice he did his best to support the Communist Party." The rebuttal to Gingrich would have been ruined. Yet that is the truth about Saul Alinsky.

And here is the truth about Barack Obama. He was trained by Alinsky's disciples; he mastered Alinsky's thought; he taught Alinsky's techniques; he funded Alinsky's acolytes, who in turn sponsored his political career; he's maintained unbroken ties with his Alinskyite mentors; and now he's using the powers of the presidency to fulfill their Alinskyite dream of abolishing the suburbs. In short, Barack Obama is a Saul Alinsky radical.

While the circumstances of Obama's career all point to his immersion in Alinskyite radicalism and the regionalist crusade, it is possible to probe still deeper. We can recover Obama's own thinking about the place of suburbs and cities in American life because we have his own words as a guide. Although it has never been properly recognized, Obama's famous memoir, *Dreams from My Father*, is in many ways a record of his early regionalist views. So let us now turn to Obama's writings, where we will discover that the antisuburban crusade isn't just one more issue for the president but the goal that lies closest to his heart.

CHAPTER FIVE

A SUBURB OF THE MIND

S uburbs are for sellouts. That is a large and overlooked theme of
Barack Obama's *Dreams from My Father*. The book is ostensibly about Obama's search for his racial identity, yet *Dreams* has
plenty to say about class. In Obama's eyes, being politically hip
means repudiating a middle-class lifestyle, symbolized by suburbia,
and identifying instead with the urban poor. Obama shares the
left's cultural bias against the bourgeois suburbs ("bourgeois," as in
property-owning, middle class, and tacky). And along with his
community organizer colleagues, Obama goes beyond mere con-
descension. For Obama, the suburbs are a defect in the very structure of American life. That is why the president backs his old friends'
movement to abolish them. It's clear from *Dreams* that anything
less would be a betrayal of Obama's most cherished ideals.

REMEMBER YOUR DREAMS

The drama in *Dreams from My Father* that turns around the contest between city and suburb has gone largely unnoticed. Many

standout moments of the book—Obama's college activism, his conversion by Jeremiah Wright, even his early years in Indonesia—hinge on a choice between city and suburb as political paths and ways of life. His little digs at sprawl have also been overlooked, as when Obama decries a Waikiki jammed with "subdivisions marching relentlessly into every fold of green hill."[1] *Dreams* actually begins with a tale of African Americans who've moved from city to suburb, for safety and better schools.[2] They suffer second thoughts as their young son runs up against prejudice, and Obama is exquisitely sensitive to their plight. Yet the moral of the story in *Dreams* is always the same: however seductive the suburb, just say no.

The suburbs are seductive, soft, and easy, but they eat the soul, thinks Obama. A man of integrity resists their invitation, even if he happens to be a fan of that ultimate suburban pastime: golf.[3] Obama's lifelong ambivalence toward the suburbs has never disappeared. *Dreams from My Father* revolves on this axis. Some part of him still wants what the suburbs have to offer, yet what he sees as his better angels call him back to the cityscape. Those better angels aren't all figurative. Obama acquired his love/hate relationship with the suburbs from his first true mentor, the poet Frank Marshall Davis.

Obama begins his memoir with a confession. He feels a bit ashamed at the innocence of his early upbringing.[4] American blacks who grow up in rough-and-tumble cities like Chicago and Gary, Indiana, cannot know the sweet naiveté of the life he lived, says Obama, reared by a white mother and grandparents in multicultural Hawaii. You can almost see Obama cringing as he recalls the Manhattan publisher who "helpfully" reminded him that he hadn't come from "an underprivileged background."[5] Obama more than half wishes that he had. Much of *Dreams* features its hero trying to banish his innocence by immersing himself in inner-city life. It's been noted that this is Obama working hard to shore up his tenuous racial identity. Yet his inner-city adventure is also an attempt to exit what he sees as the blind and dangerous "innocence" of American middle-class life.

Dreams gets under way with Obama's tracing the footsteps of his mother's parents, Stanley and Madelyn Dunham, who came from "the dab-smack, landlocked center of the country, a place where decency and endurance and the pioneer spirit were joined at the hip with conformity and suspicion and the potential for unblinking cruelty."[6] He also turns his skeptical eye toward the men of his grandfather's generation, who admired "freedom and individualism and the open road without always knowing its price."[7] Men of that time, says Obama, were "both dangerous and promising precisely because of their fundamental innocence."[8] So Obama is wary of what we might call the American dream values of individual freedom and self-betterment, values that settled the Great Plains and that live on today in the quest for a freestanding home in the suburbs. To Obama, American middle-class life is "blind to the price" of freedom and prosperity, a price paid, he implies, by the urban poor.

SHELTERED OPULENCE

Oddly enough, the best place to begin unraveling Obama's take on America's suburbs may be the time he spent from ages six to ten in Jakarta, the capital and largest city of Indonesia. He moved there with his mother, Stanley Ann Dunham, during the early years of her marriage to Lolo Soetoro, a foreign student she'd met at college, after her marriage to Barack Obama, Sr., had broken up.

Obama's treatment of those years is a study in contrasts between the bustling, gritty energy of Indonesia, on the one hand, and the sterile, sheltered opulence of the American Embassy and its environs, on the other. The home Obama and his mother first shared with Lolo was a child's wonderland: a miniature zoo, with a pet ape, two baby crocodiles, and chickens and ducks running every which way. Just getting to the house through the teeming city streets was an adventure. Obama's life with Lolo was an encounter with harsh realities: gnarled beggars; learning how to fight; slaughtering the chicken you'd have for dinner. Nestled in comfortable Hawaii, says Obama, "My grandparents knew nothing about such a world."[9]

Likewise, at the American Embassy in Jakarta, where Obama's mother worked teaching English to Indonesian businessmen, "the clamor of the street was replaced by the steady rhythm of gardening clippers. . . . The air in the office was cool and dry, like the air of mountain peaks: the pure and heady breeze of privilege."[10] The wealthy Jakarta neighborhood nearby, "where the diplomats and generals lived in sprawling houses with tall wrought-iron gates," may have been urban,[11] yet in the context of *Dreams*, that wealthy, sheltered neighborhood was a suburb of the mind, walled off from the dangerous but far more real and exciting city.

Obama compares this wealthy neighborhood with the United States. The oppressive power of the pampered and walled-off rich is nakedly obvious in Indonesia, says Obama. Yet that same power exists in America, he tells us, even if its oppressiveness is far more cleverly disguised.[12] Most Americans would see the openness to entry of America's vast middle class as proof that our country is not at all like an underdeveloped third world nation, dominated by a few oppressive rich. Yet Obama sees America's broad middle class as a cleverly disguised version of the grindingly oppressive "power" he encountered at our Indonesian embassy and its environs.

In Obama's telling, it was Lolo's embrace of a proxy version of the American dream that pulled their new family apart. Lolo got a job with an American oil company. "We moved to a house in a better neighborhood; a car replaced the motorcycle; a television and hi-fi replaced the crocodiles and Tata, the ape; Lolo could sign for our dinners at a company club."[13] This more prosperous life was not what Obama's mother wanted, however. Lolo had thought that by providing more for his family and working with an American company, he would please his new wife. Yet Obama's mother wanted nothing to do with the "ugly American" company types who frequented the embassy, and she taught her son to disdain them as well.[14] Lolo had bought into an American-made dream of success, just as his wife and son were yearning to get away from all that. Obama's mother was a romantic who idealized third world authenticity. When Lolo went upscale, she bolted.

Obama returned to the United States ahead of his mother, who spent years as an anthropologist in Indonesia. Now he was to be raised for a time by his grandparents, who met him at the airport in Hawaii. It was while driving with them along a sprawl-filled highway, "past fast-food restaurants and economy motels and used-car lots strung with festoons," that Obama first realized he'd been forced to live with strangers, for that is what his grandparents had become to him.[15] His sense of not belonging only grew when he encountered classmates at the prestigious Punahou School, who'd been together since kindergarten and who lived in the same neighborhoods, in "split-level homes with swimming pools."[16] Each of his grandparents cherished a private dream, his grandfather of a modern house "with push-button conveniences and terraced landscaping" and his grandmother of "a house with a white picket fence," where having quit her job at the bank, she could spend her days baking, playing bridge, or volunteering.[17] Obama was off-put by these aspirations. Yet he also confessed that the pull of conventional ways was slowly growing on him: "Nested in the soft, forgiving bosom of America's consumer culture, I felt safe; it was as if I had dropped into a long hibernation."[18]

A contest was raging in Obama's soul. It was the blind, innocent sleep of American consumer culture, sprawl, and dream homes against . . . what exactly? His Indonesian interlude with Lolo? That was over now. But young Obama had just been introduced to a new sort of place and a new sort of alternative.

WAIKIKI JUNGLE

In the autumn of 1970 nine-year-old Obama was back in Hawaii from Indonesia, to visit with his grandparents and to take entrance exams at the Punahou School. On the day young Barry finished those tests, his grandfather, Stanley Dunham, drove him to meet Frank Marshall Davis for the very first time. Dawna Weatherly-Williams, who was present that day and twenty-two years old at the time, recalls that Davis, "knew Stan real well. They'd play Scrabble and drink and crack jokes . . . and argue. Frank always won and he was always very braggadocio about it too. It was all jocular. They didn't get polluted drunk. And Frank never really did drugs, though he and Stan would smoke pot together."[19]

Davis lived in a little cottage in the middle of the Waikiki jungle, a ramshackle area surrounded by the high-rise tourist hotels of Waikiki. The jungle was known for its sex and dope, as Davis himself emphasized.[20] It was also a racial melting pot, with a few blacks, many whites, and a large admixture of native Hawaiians and immigrants from across the Pacific. There were also plenty of young people or, in Davis's words, members of the "now generation."

As Davis put it in a 1974 interview, "At my pad, where I live in the Cottages, I have a front porch and my pad is a sort of meeting area, kind of a town hall to an extent, for this particular section of the jungle. On any night you might find a number of people there. I may be the only Black person present."[21] Kathryn Waddell Takara, an admirer of Davis's and a scholarly expert on his life and work, described the crowd at Davis's place as a combination of hippies, young radicals, nonconformists, runaways, revolutionaries, and street hustlers.[22]

Obama described his early interactions with Davis like this: "He would read us his poetry whenever we stopped by his house, sharing whiskey with Gramps out of an emptied jelly jar. As the night wore on, the two of them would solicit my help in composing dirty limericks. Eventually, the conversation would turn to laments about women."[23]

Davis's membership in the Communist Party and his marriage to a white woman, Helen Canfield, had driven him to leave Chicago and seek refuge in Hawaii in 1948, although he had likely left the Communist Party long before meeting young Obama.[24] That Davis's poetry and general outlook remained thoroughly radical is not in doubt, however. As Takara described his waning years in Hawaii, "Davis dared to talk back, to make himself heard, to risk punishment. He remained on the left in word and deed, intention and execution. . . . He did not seek the safety of acceptable topics; he would not be silenced."[25] Davis divorced Canfield, moved to the Waikiki jungle in 1969, and completed his autobiography, *Livin' the Blues*, in the early seventies (just as he was beginning to receive visits from Obama).[26] In 1973 and 1974, during his period of contact with Obama, Davis was rediscovered and lionized by the black power movement as "the long lost father of modern Black poetry."[27]

As a practical matter, Davis was just about the only adult available to help solidify Obama's sense of being an African American male during his teenage years. We also know from Weatherly-Williams that Davis willingly embraced this role.[28] So the question is, How did Frank Marshall Davis understand black identity?

BITTER

Frank Marshall Davis opens his autobiography with an agonized and agonizing account of his graduation from high school. Davis grew up in Arkansas City, Kansas, in an era when its schools were newly integrated yet the town as a whole was not. This bright young man was an above-average student and already, at age seventeen, was six feet one and 190 pounds. Yet he felt "more like one foot six," for inferiority, he says, had been "hammered into me."[29] Shunned by white students outside school, Davis was desperate to prove himself: "[I] ran spiritually with the racist white herd, a pitiful black tag-a-long. But I ran disturbed. I had done my best to conform to white standards as I knew them. Silently I begged for acceptance by trying to prove I was not like Those Others."[30] This worked only well enough to convince Davis that he was above his fellow blacks, who derided him and the other black high school graduates with taunts of "Niggers ain't shit!"[31] These insults only confirmed Davis's disdain for others of his own race: "I *know* I am superior to Negroes reared in Dixie for they have not attended school with whites. I view them with contempt; they are *my* inferiors."[32] Yet no matter how hard young Davis tried to "act white," to whites he was still just "a big nigger kid tolerated only because state law said we must be tolerated."[33] As Davis summarizes his dilemma, ". . . emotionally I am graduating magna cum laude in bitterness. My twelve years of public schooling have taught me to be white. But I am black. And those who taught me to be white at the same time reject me because of my blackness. . . . Meanwhile I have rejected the shabby shack of the only black world I know. I am suspended uncertainly in that limbo between white and black, not yet knowing who I am."[34]

Strangely enough, the man who served as young Obama's black role model, an archetype of black radicalism and arguably the poet who first popularized the use of the word "black" instead of "Negro," was himself uncertain of his own black identity. These anguished themes recur throughout Davis's life and work.

Davis resolved his own racial identity crisis through politics. His 1975 poem "Black American," for example, surely heard by young Obama, describes an archetypical black American who is "Biologically mixed but ideologically Black."[35] The poem is filled with rage against whites and capitalism, yet the core theme is that true blackness is proved through political radicalism.

Davis moved to Chicago after his childhood on the Great Plains. Much of his poetry is an ode to that city. "By contrast with the raw, savage strength of Chicago," Davis says in his memoir, "I looked upon New York as a slick sissy."[36] In his poem "Five Portraits of Chicago at Night," Davis adds, "My city dares the weak sissy cities to come out in the yard and fight."[37] Davis opened his very first collection with "Chicago's Congo," his best poem. The piece is built around powerful juxtapositions of black Chicago and Africa.[38] Obama must have been transfixed by Chicago's Congo, especially because it was interlaced with themes of mixed blood and African ancestry.

Organizing was another frequent Davis theme. Describing the blacks of Chicago's South Side prior to the Depression, for example, Davis says that "except for churches they were generally unorganized."[39] Given his extensive work in Hawaii supporting a Communist-dominated CIO union, Davis regularly thought in these terms: who's organized and who's not. Davis's wife had been a Communist-connected neighborhood organizer in Chicago before she left with him for Hawaii.[40] Kathryn Takara, the scholar (and admirer) who worked with Davis for fifteen years in

Hawaii, has suggested that Obama first heard about organizing from his early mentor. "[Davis] talked a lot about organizing and social justice. I'm sure [Obama] was hearing that," she says.[41]

Both Frank Marshall Davis and Barack Obama were uprooted from their communities. Davis was suspended between the white and black worlds, belonging fully to neither. Obama was a young man without any clear racial, ethnic, or religious identity. His father was gone. His mother was a skeptical anthropologist, who by profession cultivated distance from her own community and serial identification with others. For both men, leftist politics and an acute sense of the world's injustice provided a way back to the feeling of racial-ethnic belonging they'd lost and beyond that to a sense of participation in the worldwide crusade for justice.

Although that leftist crusade was universal, it had a location of sorts—above all, in the ramshackle urban huddles of the world's poor. The left's crusade also had an obvious enemy in the luxurious urban redoubts of the rich. Yet it faced as well a more devious and frustrating foe in the supposedly blinkered, complacent, and tasteless suburban haunts of America's middle class. Obama knew which side he was on. Or did he?

SPANISH TILE

As Obama prepared to leave Hawaii for Occidental College, outside Los Angeles, Davis warned him against compromise. "They'll train you to want what you don't need," said Davis, as reported by Obama himself in *Dreams*. "They'll train you so good, you'll start believing what they tell you about equal opportunity and the American way and all that shit. They'll give you a corner office and invite you to fancy dinners, and tell you you're a credit to your race."[42] Obama initially recounts this warning with an eye roll, calling both Davis and his mother "incurable" for living in Hawaii's "sixties time warp."[43] Yet it quickly becomes clear that Obama is doing his best to live up to Davis's injunction, given the challenges of the mainland.

It's tough to sustain your political credentials in Occidental's "tree-lined and Spanish-tiled" suburban world, Obama laments.[44] Leaving the campus by freeway, he notes, tough inner-city neighborhoods like East L.A. and South Central remain hidden behind high concrete walls. Had he grown up in neighborhoods like those, Obama reflects, escape into academic and financial success would be a badge of honor.[45] But "I was more like the black students who had grown up in the suburbs, kids whose parents had already paid the price of escape."[46]

What follows is a long and conflicted meditation on suburban blacks, students who sit with whites in the cafeteria and refuse to be defined by the color of their skin. Obama rejects their stance, dismissing it as surrender to both the "dominant culture" and "America's happy, faceless marketplace."[47] Yet he admits to seeing large pieces of himself in these suburban black students: "And that's exactly what scared me."[48]

This is the background to the famous passage of *Dreams* in which Obama says that "to avoid being mistaken for a sellout," he chose his college friends carefully, hanging out with politically active black students, foreign students, Chicanos, structural feminists, and Marxist professors.[49] Obama's radical stance in college, at first a bit of a pose but eventually a mature position, was driven by the need to reject the path of compromise; the marketplace; "the American way and all that shit," precisely the path chosen by middle-class blacks who live in the suburbs. Ultimately, Obama took his stand instead with Frank Marshall Davis and his mother, in the rambling neighborhoods of Jakarta, in the Waikiki jungle, and in Chicago's tough South Side, far away from the workaday, suburban American middle class.

By the end of his first two years at Occidental Obama had

worked out his own version of what Davis initially taught him: hard-left politics and identification with the urban poor as the solution to a racial identity crisis. That required a transfer away from Occidental's suburban campus to Columbia University, "in the heart of a true city."[50] Eventually Obama moved to the place where Davis had pieced together his own shattered identity, the hard city streets of South Chicago.

As Obama and his community organizer colleagues saw it, middle-class flight to the suburbs by both whites and blacks was at the root of the problems in South Chicago, one of the largest poverty- and crime-ridden African American areas in the country. That flight affected businesses as well as residents. "The big manufacturers had opted for well-scrubbed suburban corridors, and not even Gandhi could have gotten them to relocate near [South Chicago] anytime soon," Obama laments in *Dreams*.[51] Not even Gandhi, but perhaps a president of the United States.

OUT OF THE LINE OF FIRE

Given all the controversy over the Reverend Jeremiah Wright, it's easy to overlook the degree to which Obama's story of Wright in *Dreams* is really a tale about the suburbs. Even before Obama meets Wright, when he's simply shopping for a congregation, the issue of the suburbs dominates the future president's thinking. Obama tells the story of his encounter with a Reverend Phillips, who offers him some perspective on Chicago's historically black churches. Bad as the days of segregation were, says Phillips, there was a hidden blessing in the way it forced blacks of all income levels to worship together. Nowadays, says Phillips, most of his better-off members have moved to the suburbs. Although they drive back for Sunday services, they won't volunteer for tasks that would keep them after dark. They also ask for a fenced-in parking lot to protect their cars. Phillips expects that once he passes from the scene, his suburban congregants will start tidy new churches of their own where they live.[52] Along with Phillips, Obama regrets this.

Around this same time, Obama was readying himself to leave community organizing to enter Harvard Law School. There follows Obama's lengthy and agonized reflections about that move. Was he simply escaping to a more comfortable life, like Reverend Phillips's suburban congregants? Was he no different from the suburban black students at Occidental after all? Obama could justify decamping to Harvard only by promising himself to master the wily ways of "power" and return with this knowledge to help the inner-city poor.[53] Obviously, his fear of selling out still moved him while suburban life remained an ultimate symbol of political and cultural betrayal.

Given all we now know, it's odd to think that Obama might once have suspected Jeremiah Wright of being a sellout. Yet that is essentially what Obama tells us in *Dreams*. Wright's fast-growing church had a tremendous following among young black professionals, and some city pastors scorned it for that.[54] Obama was particularly distressed to learn that one of Wright's assistants, a young woman whose husband had just died, decided to move to the suburbs for the sake of her son's safety. She wrestled long and hard with the decision, yet Obama disapproved.[55] He also took her move as a mark against Wright.

When Obama confronted Wright with the claims that his church was "too upwardly mobile," his pastor-to-be replied: "That's a lot of bull." Obama countered with the story of Wright's assistant, bemoaning "the tendency of those with means to move out of the line of fire." Wright made it clear he had disapproved of the woman's move and had told her so himself: "That boy of hers is gonna get out there and won't have a clue about where, or who, he is." For a moment Obama tried taking the woman's side:

"It's tough to take chances with your child's safety." Wright shot back: "Life's not safe for a black man in this country, Barack. Never has been. Probably never will be."[56]

This is what Obama was hoping to hear. But what finally convinced him of Reverend Wright's political bona fides, he says, was the "Disavowal of the Pursuit of Middleclassness" written into the church's "Black Value System."[57] Obama decided that the inner-city poor in Wright's church might actually be educating all those professionals. After all, thought Obama, the struggles of the poor give them greater claims to authenticity than middle-class blacks have. The willingness of black professionals to accept that authenticity (by disavowing the symbolic authority of middle-classness) was a good start. In the end, however, the true test for Obama would be the willingness of Wright and his church to "engage with real power and risk genuine conflict."[58] In other words, as Wright himself has told us, Obama was looking to recruit Wright's church into political confrontations that he and his fellow organizers would engineer.[59]

STILL AROUND

The Jeremiah Wright connection is supposedly no longer an issue for President Obama. That was all adjudicated in 2008. What matters now instead, we're told, are the first four years of Obama's presidency. Yet we've looked at his presidency and discovered that all is not what it seems. Obama has launched a quiet "war against the suburbs" but has not been willing to frankly acknowledge it, much less discuss the full dimensions or rationale of that antisuburban crusade. It turns out that you can learn at least as much about the fate of America's suburbs in a possible second Obama term by reading *Dreams from My Father* as by attending to what the president actually says, maybe more.

Reverend Wright still haunts the Obama presidency, far more than the public realizes. Wright, by the way, has a history of co-operation with Obama's regionalist colleagues at the Gamaliel Foundation.[60] Much less has changed than Obama and his supporters would have us believe. Yet the continuing influence of Obama's past goes far beyond his years with Wright. We've seen that the preoccupations that brought young Obama to his controversial pastor were of long standing. Obama's relationship with Wright was merely the culmination of a lifetime spent disavowing middle-class "suburbanness" and identifying instead with the urban poor. All along, in Obama's own telling, his goal has been to grasp the ways of power and turn those techniques to an ultimate disavowal of middle-classness. What better way for a master of power to prove his authenticity than to abolish the suburbs themselves? Let someone try to call that a sellout! In some other-worldly Waikiki jungle, the ghost of Frank Marshall Davis is smiling.

CHAPTER SIX

REDISTRIBUTION REVOLUTION

An American will build a house in which to pass his old age and sell it before the roof is on; he will plant a garden and rent it just as the trees are coming into bearing; he will clear a field and leave others to reap the harvest; he will take up a profession and leave it, settle in one place and soon go off elsewhere with his changing desires.[1]

S o says Alexis de Tocqueville, one of the great philosophers of liberal democracy and history's most penetrating observer of American society. For Tocqueville, a Frenchman writing from 1835 to 1850, the restless desire to better our circumstances and our willingness to pick up stakes and move to make it happen are built into the American character. Our immigrant origins and our continent's frontier vastness have made it so. More deeply, America's commitment to equality and freedom nurtures a faith in our capacity to better ourselves and inspires the willingness to try. What looks to Obama and his regionalist allies like middle-class flight to the suburbs is really the restless democratic spirit so brilliantly described by Tocqueville some 170 years ago.

In previous chapters I've traced the president's efforts to advance the regionalist agenda. Now it's time to take a closer look at the agenda itself, focusing on the writings of the leaders of the movement for regional equity, who also happen to be strategic partners of the Gamaliel Foundation and Building One America and key participants in the recent White House forum on the suburbs. (Two of those leaders also advise the Obama administration.) We'll draw on critics of regionalism as well. The greatest critic of all, however, was Tocqueville, who knew nothing of the movement for regional equity, yet refuted its premises long ago just by explaining what makes America tick.

OBAMA VERSUS TOCQUEVILLE

As the child is father to the man, Tocqueville believed that America's distinctive traits were present from the moment of its Pilgrim origins. The Puritans came from the heart of England's middle classes, said Tocqueville. Neither uneducated peasants nor wealthy aristocrats, they had the ability to govern themselves and took human equality for granted. Left unmolested by an English government content to be rid of them, the Puritans were free to manage their own affairs. So instead of political orders from a monarchy filtering down to the local level, government in America began with the tiny township and spread upward from there over time to the county, the state, and ultimately the Union.[2]

Tocqueville feared the despotism of centralized government, which he identified with monarchies of the past and a possible socialism of the future. That's why he cherished America's tradition of local self-government, which he saw as the ultimate guarantor of liberty. To Tocqueville, America's lack of a great and influential national capital was a boon to freedom. Yet if a bloated and powerful Washington was no threat to America when Tocqueville visited in the 1830s, the growing size of Philadelphia and New York worried him. Tocqueville warned that the as yet unassimilated immigrants and the impoverished and uneducated ex-slaves huddled together in America's growing cities would take time to embrace the middle-class spirit of enterprise that is America's salvation. This was a significant challenge to democracy, he believed. Tocqueville suggested that if America's spirit of free self-government were ever to be killed off, massive cities desperate for a centralized welfare state would strike the deadly blow.[3]

Tocqueville told the story of how the state of Connecticut, which formed only a forty-third part of the United States in 1830, was birthplace to a full eighth of the members of Congress that year. Connecticut itself had only five members in its congressional delegation, yet it was the birth state of thirty-one congressmen representing other states. Were it not for America's frontier and its tradition of restless movement, said Tocqueville, those thirty-one congressmen—all now credits to their communities and prosperous holders of property in states far from their places of birth—would have piled up in eastern cities, some of them likely becoming poor and even dangerous citizens.[4] Tocqueville marveled that the state of Ohio, whose capital hadn't yet been in existence for thirty years, was already sending settlers into the fertile prairies of Illinois.[5] This never-ending outward movement and the enterprising attitude that powered it, said Tocqueville, were the secrets of America's prosperity and peace.

"In Europe," he added, "we habitually regard a restless spirit, immoderate desire for wealth, and an extreme love of independence as great social dangers. But precisely those things assure a long and peaceful future for the American republics."[6] In other words, the same ethic of individual enterprise that comes off as vulgar materialism to many Europeans is the key to our civil harmony. So long as the spirit of self-improvement is in, Euro-style class warfare is out. In keeping with this reversal, Tocqueville commented on how differently Americans and Europeans see the world: "What we call love of gain is praiseworthy industry to the Americans, and they see something of a cowardly spirit in what we consider moderation of desires."[7] Europeans also find it admirable that a man should live a lifetime in the place of his birth, said Tocqueville, which strikes Americans as peculiar.

If someone in 1835 had proposed that Washington, D.C., promulgate a series of regulations forcing Americans out of the frontier and back into cities or had said that tiny townships ought to be swallowed up by regional megagovernments, at the command of state legislatures and with the connivance of the president, and then had claimed that all this was necessary to solve the problem of urban poverty, Tocqueville would have been first dumbstruck, then horrified. The plan would have seemed to him the epitome of despotism and the antithesis of the American spirit. Yet this is essentially what the movement long supported by Obama is proposing.

Obama and his regionalist allies take urban poverty to be a product of flight to the suburbs. That poverty, thinks Obama, is the unacknowledged price of America's penchant for "freedom and individualism and the open road."[8] Yet Tocqueville saw the restless drive to better one's condition by ceaseless movement outward as the most effective antipoverty program the world had ever known.

The regionalists' reply to this is that Tocqueville's America is gone, and the suburbs are not the frontier. The regionalist guru and Obama administration adviser Bruce Katz argues that the America of Thomas Jefferson, dominated by small towns and countryside, has disappeared and that the new urbanized and globally interconnected world demands that America be restructured as a collection of regional governments, just like those increasingly found in Europe.[9]

The economic necessity of regional governance is far from established. Arguments like Katz's serve as cover for pushing America toward a Euro-style centralized, redistributive welfare state, the very "soft despotism" Tocqueville warned against.[10] While the United States may no longer be dominated by small towns and farms, most Americans do live in suburbs, places where the restless spirit of enterprise and independence described by Tocqueville remains very much alive.

SUBURBAN SUPERNOVA

The features of Tocqueville's frontier are easy to catch sight of in *The Paradise Suite,* the *New York Times* columnist David Brooks's wise and witty 2005 study of the suburbs today.[11] Americans still move around more than any other people on earth, Brooks tells us, proving with statistics what Tocqueville intuited in the 1830s.[12] What Brooks calls our suburban supernova of population decentralization has the nonstop, spillover feel of America's original frontier: "The people who were in move out, and the people who were out move farther out, into the suburbs of suburbia."[13] Brooks might as well be talking about freshly settled Ohioans pushing out to virgin land in Illinois in the 1830s.

Earlier we caught the leading regionalist Bruce Katz going after Sarah Palin's supposed village idiocy.[14] Katz wants Palin to think of herself not as a countrified, moose-hunting mama grizzly but as a citified metro mama, all because about a third of the workers in the Alaskan borough (county) in which her hometown of Wasilla sits commute to Anchorage (itself almost a small town by lower forty-eight standards). What about the other two-thirds? It's a question that applies to suburbs as well as small towns. Today's suburbanites increasingly work at nearby office parks, forgoing urban commutes altogether. Brooks shows that suburbs nowadays are less bedroom communities revolving around some urban center than increasingly untethered places of their own.[15] Regionalists cannot give this new reality its due. On the contrary, their numbers games are designed to pump up suburban dependency while playing down local autonomy.

Brooks himself links our modern suburban supernova to America's frontier days. Land speculation was so feverish back in the 1770s, he tells us, ministers complained that congregations could no longer be kept together.[16] That puts us in mind of no one so much as Reverend Phillips of Obama's *Dreams from My Father*, bemoaning his middle-class congregants' departure for the suburbs, with Obama and Jeremiah Wright echoing his protest. Yet Brooks suggests that the exodus neither can nor should be stopped.

Brooks's *The Paradise Suite* is ultimately a defense of America's character, as embodied in the spirit of our suburbs. Even the most sympathetic students of America's vast middle classes—Tocqueville included—have convicted them of a certain superficiality. Brooks argues instead that America's enterprising middle-class suburbanites are driven less by need or greed than by an "everyday utopianism," a secular-spiritual drive to transcend and redeem through singular individual achievement.[17]

When Europeans aren't busy turning up their noses at American vulgarity, says Brooks, they see our frontier as a paradise filled with gold and diamonds for the taking, "an Eldorado to be looted." Even secular Americans, by contrast, he says, see our suburban frontier more spiritually, as "an Eden to be occupied."[18] By this reckoning, Obama and his community organizer buddies look at America's suburbs through European eyes. They see the tax money of middle-class suburban achievers as an Eldorado to be looted and redistributed to the cities. As for suburbs as an

Eden to be occupied, Obama and his pals play God, casting the sinners out.

FULL SPEED AHEAD

The suburbs are a product of America's distinctive spirit of freedom and enterprise. Paradoxically, however, the special place of suburbs in America also reflects a widespread human desire to burst out of overcrowded cities to find space and independence beyond. What distinguishes America is the wide berth that our vast continent and traditions of free movement and enterprise have given to this much more general human tendency.

Understanding the ancient and widespread human urge to seek less dense living space on the outskirts of cities is important because regionalists often deny that America's suburbs are an authentic expression of public choice, treating them as products of government intervention instead. Regionalists claim that policies like single-use zoning and the mortgage interest deduction on federal income taxes somehow lured Americans away from the cities when they would otherwise have stayed in town. Regionalists also attribute the suburbs to technological innovations like the automobile and to federal highway building as well. The implication is that if government policies once forced people out of the cities and into the suburbs, there's nothing wrong with government policies designed to force the public back to the cities today.

Yet regionalist claims about the origins of the suburbs are mistaken, as Robert Bruegmann powerfully establishes in his study *Sprawl: A Compact History*.[19] Moving from settlements on the outskirts of ancient Rome through the development of Europe to modern America, Bruegmann shows that across history so-called sprawl—movement outward from cities into less dense residential

developments—has been the preferred settlement pattern any-
where citizens enjoyed a degree of affluence and freedom. In
short, people all over the world and across history have actively
chosen to live in suburbs. What makes America distinctive is that
our economic and political system provides citizens with the
wherewithal to exercise that choice.

Bruegmann also shows that American downtowns were on the
decline well before the post–World War II suburban explosion
and that the regionalists' scapegoating of suburbs for the problems of the central cities is vastly exaggerated. Cars, adds Bruegmann, didn't so much do in public transportation as they replaced
carriages, giving ordinary middle-class citizens the privacy, mobility, and choice that luxury transportation had once afforded
only to the wealthy. Americans who could afford it began moving
to the suburbs long before World War II. What changed after the
war, Bruegmann shows, is that prosperity enabled middle-class
Americans to do what only wealthy folks in search of space and
privacy had been capable of before them.

In short, government policies didn't create the suburbs. The
prosperity generated by American's tradition of individual liberty
and its system of free enterprise did that. Government simply gave
a bit of extra help to a citizenry already barreling full speed ahead
toward the suburbs.

A JEREMIAH WRIGHT PROBLEM

So much for America's spirit of freedom and enterprise. It's time
to consider the writings of our country's leading regionalist
thinkers, who turn that tradition on its head. We'll devote particular attention to john a. powell, David Rusk, and Myron Orfield, longtime strategic partners of both the Gamaliel Foundation

and Building One America and featured speakers at Building One America's White House forum on the suburbs.

It's a near certainty that as a voracious reader who devoured anything at all related to community organizing during his years in New York and Chicago, Obama is familiar with the work of the intellectual leaders of the regionalist movement. After all, he funded and supported that movement for years, and his cherished Gamaliel mentors were deeply committed to the cause.

In May 2008, at the height of the controversy over Barack Obama's relationship to his pastor Jeremiah Wright, William Schambra, a fellow at Washington, D.C.'s conservative Hudson Institute (with which I was once affiliated), published a widely noticed article in the *Chronicle of Philanthropy*.[20] There Schambra argues that philanthropy has a "Jeremiah Wright problem." Americans might be surprised to learn, he says, that grants from some of the nation's most prestigious foundations support activists who hold views much like those of Wright. According to Schambra, adherents of the theory of structural racism use grants from places like the Tides Center and the Annie E. Casey, Charles Stewart Mott, W. K. Kellogg, Rockefeller, and Ford foundations to spread their claim that America is "riven by an unrelenting and deeply oppressive racial divide." Devotees of this theory, says Schambra, claim that the only way to be rid of structural racism is to institute "dramatic, perhaps revolutionary" changes designed to "introduce complete equality to all aspects of our national life."

Schambra's piece brings to mind Mike Kruglik's proud boast that the Gamaliel Foundation is "battling apartheid in America" because that quote comes from a study conducted by a consortium of liberal foundations (including Mott, Rockefeller, Ford, and Annie E. Casey).[21] That same foundation-produced document praises the regional equity movement and makes frequent reference to the work of the Gamaliel strategic partner john a. powell.[22] As a leader of the Structural Racism Caucus, powell joined with his colleagues in sending a letter to the *Chronicle of Philanthropy* replying to Schambra and defending the concept of structural racism.[23]

By partnering with Building One America and having john powell speak at the White House, President Obama is supporting a movement whose ideology echoes Wright's.

Barack Obama may not proclaim his determination to transform the United States into a European-style social democracy, but john powell does. Powell is a fan of Jeremy Rifkin's book *The European Dream: How Europe's Vision of the Future Is Quietly Eclipsing the American Dream*.[24] Rifkin is periodically invoked in powell's writings and lectures, in a way that makes powell's preference for the European social model very clear.

You can see powell's transformative vision most clearly in his essay "Moving Beyond the Isolated Self."[25] There, drawing on Rifkin, powell attacks the "American self" and its associated ideas of private property and market capitalism as much too "isolated and separate." Powell prefers the more "inter-connected" European self, embodied, for example, in the Continent's shared currency, the euro. (Obviously powell was writing before the recent euro crisis.) From the standpoint of the theory of structural racism, powell argues that the problem with "whiteness" in America is its close identification with the far too separate and egoistic Western self. He is essentially saying that the only way to overcome the structural defects of American whiteness is to adopt the ethic of interconnectedness and mutual responsibility embodied in European social democracy. In a nutshell, Euro socialism is powell's cure for America's so-called structural racism.

Among regionalist thinkers, powell is easily the most focused on the issue of race. Remarkably, however, even for him structural racism ends up having more to do with questions of capitalism versus socialism than with race per se. It's all as Schambra explains in "Philanthropy's Jeremiah Wright Problem." In fact, when you probe Wright's history and writings, socialist sympathies turn out to be the bottom line of his approach to race too.[26]

In his PowerPoint presentation at the White House forum on the suburbs, powell was careful not to bring his radicalism too far to the fore.[27] There was a mention of whiteness, for example, but without significant explanation. He also floated the controversial redistributionist idea of regional tax base sharing, yet only briefly. If you know his broader writings, however, the direction in which powell wants to push this new movement is obvious.

To be sure, powell's views are radical, and he was less than up front about that at the White House forum. Yet in his broader body of work powell is more frank than his colleagues. In framing the regionalist battle as a contest of ultimate societal values—American free market capitalism versus European social democracy—powell gets the alternatives right. His regionalist colleagues, on the other hand, President Obama very much included, drive awareness of that choice underground at every opportunity.

WITHOUT CONSENT OF THE GOVERNED

Take David Rusk, a former civil rights and antipoverty worker with the Washington Urban League, the mayor of Albuquerque, New Mexico, from 1977 to 1981, and a longtime adviser to the Gamaliel Foundation and Building One America and now, to the Obama administration as well.[28] It's clear from his 1993 book *Cities Without Suburbs* that Rusk's real goal is to abolish the suburbs.[29] For Rusk, the ideal way to achieve this is annexation, the swallowing up of suburbs by a central city, without consent of the governed. A combination of growth boundaries (to force suburbanites back into cities), low-income housing quotas (to force the urban poor out to the suburbs), and regional tax base sharing (to transfer suburban wealth to cities) will do for Rusk in a pinch, effectively wiping out any differences between cities and suburbs over time.[30] Yet Rusk's preference for outright annexation is clear.

In 2003, a decade after publishing his bold case for doing away with suburbs, Rusk offered a thought about regionalist political strategy: "The policy debate must be framed not as a choice between conservative and liberal philosophies, but as a choice between policies that work and policies that do not work."[31]

The swallowing up of suburbs by cities or by newly established regional governments (which amounts to the same thing) would signal a profound rejection of America's most cherished traditions of self-government. If there was ever a stark choice between liberal and conservative philosophies—American and European approaches—this is it. Yet adopting the rhetorical strategy favored by Obama himself, Rusk would portray this revolutionary shift of ideals as a merely pragmatic decision. Rusk's claims about what works and what doesn't when it comes to urban policy are questionable, to say the least. His policy answers stem not from pragmatic calculations but from his own redistributionist values.

From *The Federalist Papers* through Tocqueville to the present, the essence of American democracy has been embodied in the practice of individual liberty, voluntary association, and self-government. To anyone who reveres that tradition, Rusk's talk of annexation should be anathema. Rusk sings the praises of state annexation laws that operate "regardless of property owners' desires" and bemoans the many state laws that require an affirmative vote of affected landowners instead.[32] Placing a city's expansion "at the mercy" of suburban residents is Rusk's idea of bad policy.[33] He even dismisses referenda on regional consolidation as ill-advised "invitations to opposition" from urban minority politicians, generally every bit as sour on regionalism as suburbanites, white and black.[34]

Rusk certainly doesn't come off as a fan of freedom or democracy. He thirsts for redistribution by fiat: "Poorer communities have no way of tapping the wealth of richer communities without the intervention of a higher level of government."[35] Rusk is out to annex your suburb and pick your pocket. If annoying principles like individual liberty, voluntary association, and self-government stand in his way, that's just too bad. The contradiction between hard-left redistributionism and traditional American freedoms could hardly be drawn more sharply.

True, annexation was practiced by some American cities in the nineteenth century, back when there was no other good way for growing towns to hook up to basic infrastructure.[36] As that changed, states rightly began to forbid annexation without the consent of the governed. Nor does the nineteenth-century experience prove the regionalist case. Consider Chicago, one of the cities that grew through annexation during the 1800s. De facto segregation and concentrated poverty, the very problems regionalists claim they're out to solve, are nowhere more severe than in Chicago.[37] Consolidating local tax bases didn't solve the problems of Obama's hometown.

ELASTIC ILLUSION

That brings us to Rusk's core claim about what works when it comes to urban policy. Rusk argues that "elastic" cities—cities that expand to annex or consolidate with nearby suburbs—do better economically than do "inelastic" cities—that is, cities that remain sharply separate from their surrounding municipalities.[38]

Critics have argued persuasively that Rusk's evidence for this claim is largely a statistical artifact.[39] Let's say you have a city and a nearby suburban area of equal population. Now suppose people in the city have an average income of fifteen thousand dollars while folks in the surrounding suburbs have an average income of twenty-five thousand dollars. Let the city annex its suburbs, and the average urban income immediately shoots up to twenty thousand dollars. Yet nothing has actually changed; the "improvement" is an illusion. Any subsequent growth in the city's average income has to be calculated separately from the increase automatically created by the annexation itself. Rusk fails to make that separation. Rusk also compares newly growing nonmanufacturing cities with older manufacturing-based cities during a period of manufacturing decline, and state capitals with nonstate capitals in a time of government growth.[40] Adjust for these factors and compare entire metropolitan areas, and most of Rusk's annexation advantages disappear.

Critics have also hit Rusk for failing to take into account the public choice perspective on local government, championed by thinkers like Charles M. Tiebout.[41] Public choice theorists draw on the philosophy of local governance laid down by Alexander Hamilton and James Madison in *The Federalist Papers* and elaborated later by Tocqueville.[42] They argue that competition between a wide range of local governments offering different services and tax policies increases efficiency, encourages public participation, keeps taxes low, and generally provides Americans with greater choice about how they want to live.

Rusk gives these arguments short shrift but in fact concedes a number of points. He admits, for example, that "[g]iven the bureaucratic impulse of many large systems, a Metro government may be less efficient and less responsive as a deliverer of services than smaller governments."[43] And although he's silent on the issue, Rusk likely agrees with those who say competition between local governments keeps taxes low. Then why doesn't he say so? Probably because higher taxes and more redistribution are exactly what he wants: "How can responsibility for poor minorities be made a metropolitanwide responsibility?"[44] This is Rusk's real aim, and he's willing to sacrifice our traditions of voluntary association, local self-government, and the goals of efficiency and frugality to get there. Rusk's "pragmatic" arguments don't stand up to scrutiny, but why should he care? He's guided, after all, by his redistributionist political ideology.

Talk about policies that don't work: Rusk touts Fannie Mae and Freddie Mac as models for spreading low-income housing to America's middle-class suburbs.[45] Just as Fannie and Freddie gave special breaks on home loans to low-income people with shaky credit histories, so Rusk wants homeowners in suburbs who build low-income housing to get a break on their mortgages. Rusk suggested this before Fannie and Freddie went under in the financial meltdown of 2008. It turns out that seemingly pain-free redistributionism can be dangerous to your economic health.

The PowerPoint presentation Rusk offered to participants in Building One America's White House forum on the suburbs doesn't raise the issue of annexation.[46] Instead Rusk lays out only the short-term goals of the regionalist agenda, explaining, for example, how federal funds can be used as carrots in conjunction with the administration's Sustainable Communities Initiative. Since Rusk has been working with the Obama administration for several years on that program, he knows whereof he speaks.[47] Rusk's participation in the White House forum was not some passing, one-of-a-kind event but part of President Obama's concerted effort to establish the views of Gamaliel and its leading advisers as national policy. The more you know about Rusk's long-term goals and underlying principles, the more worrisome that is.

DANGER RED

The third member of the trio of strategic partners long associated with the Gamaliel Foundation and its new offshoot, Building One America, and now an adviser to the Obama administration is University of Minnesota law professor Myron Orfield. David Rusk calls Orfield "the most revolutionary politician in urban America."[48] He lauds Orfield for having politically "split the suburbs" around Minneapolis–St. Paul so as to put regional tax base sharing in place.[49] Inherently divisive proposals like tax base sharing, says Rusk, aren't advanced through "friendly, consensual agreement."[50] Political hardball is required if a coalition of the have-nots is going to wrestle local tax revenues away from the haves. Orfield knows how to play that game, Rusk assures us.

Orfield has devised a powerful political tool in the form of multicolored maps he uses to highlight "fiscal disparities" between various cities and suburbs.[51] The story he tells, using these maps as proof, is of a vicious, self-reinforcing cycle of decline in cities and less well-off suburbs, as prosperous suburbanites get richer. As Orfield describes it, residentially exclusive suburbs with low tax rates attract businesses, whose presence lowers tax rates even more. Less well-off suburbs, on the other hand, are forced to zone for homes of lesser value; that keeps social needs high and creates pressure for still higher taxes. Cities are caught in a version of the same trap, says Orfield.[52]

There are some serious problems with these claims, many raised, surprisingly, by the left-leaning *Chicago Reader* when Orfield came to town at the invitation of the Obama-funded Gamaliel Foundation in the mid-1990s.[53] For one thing, Orfield's maps don't actually show worsening local disparities in tax bases, crime, health, and so on. That's because they're simply snapshots in time. Orfield's multicolored maps also tend to exaggerate disparities because communities that score below average in a given category show up in danger red or orange, whereas Orfield colors municipalities that score above average in shades of benign blue. A virtually uniform region in which the wealthiest suburb had a median income of $42,005, and the poorest $41,995, would still produce a seemingly dramatic disparity between poor red suburbs and rich blue suburbs. Many suburbs rate poorly in some categories but well in others; that suggests they may not be locked into hopeless cycles of decline after all.

In general neither Rusk nor Orfield has a way of explaining improvement. When Rusk published an update of *Cities Without Suburbs* after the 2000 census, he had the problem of dealing with widespread slowdowns and reversals of the city-suburb income gap. He played down the changes, never coming to grips with the challenge they posed to his theory.[54] Similarly, in his 2002 study *American Metropolitics*, Orfield had to deal with the awkward fact of a decline in housing segregation by race during the 1990s. He tiptoed around the change, never considering that America's suburban dream may still work.[55]

COERCION AT EVERY TURN

What exactly does Orfield want? Although styled by Rusk as "the most revolutionary politician in urban America," Orfield portrays himself as a moderate. He claims to look for compromise at every turn and has said he'd be pleased with the ratio of four to one between the highest and lowest municipal tax bases in a given region. Yet he complains about three to one tax base ratios in *American Metropolitics*.[56] More important, Orfield wants to redefine municipal services as a "birthright," including what even he calls "second tier" services like parks and recreation.[57] Given that, it's tough to see any stopping point to Orfield's drive for redistribution.

Almost everywhere America has a safety net that works to equalize local school expenditures through state aid to education. Orfield acknowledges this yet waves it away as inadequate, even as he cites it as a precedent.[58] Because states already redistribute via aid to public schools, Orfield denies that his own redistributionist proposals are radical. He says the difference between regional tax base sharing and traditional state aid to education is merely one of degree, not kind.

It would be as true to say that the difference between investors holding 1 percent and those with 65 percent of stock in a company is merely one of degree. Yet in the second case, effective ownership yields the power to transform a business out of all recognition. Mere changes of degree easily reach tipping points that enable radical alterations. A man skydiving with an only slightly smaller parachute each time will eventually die. At some point, even moving by small degrees, a society based on individual freedom, enterprise, and opportunity, with a safety net for the poor and aged, morphs into a centralized, redistributive Euro-socialist welfare state. That is where we are headed, and Obama, working with allies like Orfield, means to take us there. At least john powell poses these alternatives with a modicum of frankness.

Orfield likes to claim that redistributing money from suburbs to cities is perfectly justified because governments have unfairly subsidized the growth of suburbs—by building federal highways, for example.[59] That argument is unconvincing, as we've seen. If for no other reasons than defense and public safety, the federal highway system would have been necessary to build. What really bothers Orfield is what the public has chosen to do with those highways.

Even in Europe, where governments have worked hard to prevent so-called sprawl, by enacting everything from exorbitant gas taxes to draconian development barriers, these efforts have largely failed.[60] London's urban population is now scattering across the south of England at a higher rate than suburbs are growing in America.[61] Europe's suburban supernova was delayed but not denied.

The suburbs grew up because Americans prefer affordable freestanding houses with yards, not because of government manipulation. Regionalists aren't equalizing government subsidies; they're employing coercion at every turn, telling the public where and where not to live, where and where not to drive, and raiding voters' wallets whenever possible. Give regionalists half a chance, and they'll annex your town without your consent. Liberty is not a regionalist strong suit.

But what about all those redistributed goodies? Don't they make it worthwhile to sign on to the regionalist crusade? The sympathetic chroniclers of regionalism Manuel Pastor, Jr., Chris Benner, and Martha Matsuoka explain why Orfield's tax base sharing scheme has had so little appeal outside liberal Minneapolis: ". . . immediate incentives for such regional collaboration can be scant—residents in older suburbs are as likely to contemplate their next life in the exurbs as they are to identify with and work with disadvantaged communities."[62] Traditionally Americans have been more interested in climbing the ladder of success themselves than in spreading the wealth around. Redistribution undercuts incentives for the growth that benefits all.

DIRTY LITTLE SECRET

Redistribution is the heart and soul of regionalism, yet the movement has a dirty little secret far more controversial than that. If there's one thing regionalists agree on, it's their antipathy to culture of poverty arguments.[63] Conservatives often say that the deepest cause of poverty is cultural, that persistent, intergenerational want has undercut the ethic of personal responsibility and enterprise that is the real creator of wealth in this country. Regionalists supposedly reject that argument as blaming the victim. Apparently they prefer blaming suburbanites instead.

Recall that Obama's Gamaliel colleagues embraced regionalism as a way of explaining their own failure to improve the neighborhoods they were organizing. Even when their groups managed to pry loose government money from reluctant politicians, urban conditions remained essentially the same. Regionalism gave Gamaliel's organizers a way of making sense of their failures, without rethinking their redistributive goals.[64]

Yet whether they admit it or not, regionalists actually embrace the very culture of poverty arguments they supposedly reject. Consider David Rusk's explanation of why traditional poverty programs aren't enough, why urban residents have to be forced to live in the suburbs instead: "Bad neighborhoods defeat good programs."[65] What exactly does he mean by "bad neighborhoods?"

Orfield spells out the regionalist logic more clearly. Concentrated urban poverty, he says, fosters "an oppositional culture that rejects middle-class norms and disdains the traditional value placed by the broader society on education and work."[66] He follows this up by slinging around talk about "pathologies" of the urban poor that could easily get a more conservative politician into trouble.[67] Then he adds: "Most people believe that middle-class presence is necessary for healthy, stable communities. The middle-class sets social norms. . . . However, transforming dense clusters of poor people into members of the middle-class is extraordinarily difficult through either liberal empowerment or conservative discipline-type strategies. First, poverty has to be de-concentrated."[68]

In other words, Rusk and Orfield actually do buy the conservative culture of poverty analysis. They just add that the way to solve the problem is to spread the urban poor out into the suburbs while forcing suburbanites back into the city.

The conservative urbanist Howard Husock exposes the flaw in this thinking. Regionalists, he says, imagine "that middle-class habits will rub off on the poor if government drops them into middle-class neighborhoods, rather than understanding that it is the incentive of reaching a better neighborhood that encourages the habits of thrift and industry."[69]

Regionalists want to have their cake and eat it too. They quietly root for middle-class morality to replace the culture of poverty, even as they push a resentful ethos of entitlement on the poor. Regionalists beg off public arguments that supposedly blame the victim, then expect middle-class morality to somehow magically take hold. But if leftist political leaders won't publicly speak up for the benefits of middle-class morality, why should the urban poor change their ways?

No one is more guilty of this contradiction than Barack Obama, who was using Woods Fund grants to spread the gospel of Orfield and Rusk even as he was lauding Jeremiah Wright's "Disavowing of the Pursuit of Middleclassness."[70] *Dreams from My Father* can be read as a book-length argument against conservative culture of poverty claims. In the end, however, the regionalist movement that Obama has supported from its beginnings until now actually depends upon culture of poverty premises, without having the guts to own up to it, much less follow through.

Regionalism is a cop-out. Middle-class morality doesn't rub off from mere proximity. It's the steadiness you have little choice but to adopt when you're forced to climb the ladder, reinforced when leaders in your community send a message of personal responsibility. With their cries for redistributive "social justice," Obama and his organizer buddies have undercut that vital message from day one.

Orfield's PowerPoint presentation at the White House forum on the suburbs was filled with multicolored charts and talk of local inequities, tax base sharing, and the need to organize in partnership with Kruglik's Building One America.[71] As a member of President Obama's urban and regional policy transition team and a frequent administration adviser since then, Orfield is well placed to advance his views.

This is no mere question of the president's radical Alinskyite past, although there is almost perfect continuity between Obama's organizer history and his current policies for both city and suburb. Obama is closely allied with the self-styled "most revolutionary" movement in urban America, a movement whose ultimate goal is nothing less than the abolition of the suburbs. Their policy is his policy, and always has been.

There is more than one way to do in the suburbs. The most direct route is for cities to formally annex them. In lieu of this, as we've seen, government at various levels can raid suburban tax money, then use housing, transportation, and land use regulation to force suburban residents back to the cities and city people out to the suburbs.

Yet another strategy is to go after suburban school districts. Many people move out to the suburbs in search of high-quality education, and they're willing to pay for that schooling in taxes. Seize suburban school spending and transfer it to the cities, or somehow merge urban and suburban school districts, and you will have undermined the suburbs at what is arguably their most essential point. Unbeknownst to the country at large, President Obama is aiming to do just that, as we shall learn in the following chapter.

CHAPTER SEVEN

FOOLED, RULED, AND SCHOOLED

If you live in a suburb because you like the school system, watch out. A reelected President Obama could start merging your local school district with that of a nearby city. It's all a part of his quest to abolish the suburbs. Transforming America's education system is a central focus of Obama's allies in the regional equity movement because a gradual blending of urban and suburban school systems would undermine the social basis of the suburbs: the quest for high-quality and more locally controlled schools.

Americans believe in individual freedom and self-government, and central to personal liberty and self-rule is the ability to educate your children as you see fit. Americans also believe that the drive to better your own economic situation is the key to prosperity for all. When young couples work and save so that they can move to a home in a suburb with just the sorts of schools they want for their children, we say that they are pursuing the American dream. Shut off that dream with a misguided effort to equalize the funding of every American school district, and you will take away the engine that drives our prosperity, undermining in the process the ability of parents to control what their children learn. Much of the motivation that drives young Americans to work and save will be taken away. Forced income redistribution will create an equality of the lowest common denominator in America's schools, as the drive to better your child's circumstances will be rendered pointless. And the national education system that will be necessary to manage this economic redistribution will destroy the ability of local communities to decide what their children learn. A national curriculum created and run by Obama's supporters will quickly become the only game in town. Get ready for leftist indoctrination in your children's schools.

Because Obama's top priority is the redistribution and equalization of school spending nationally, he is quietly working to seize control of your children's education. His immediate goal is to nationalize the curriculum, but that is only the run-up to a still bolder attempt to force the redistribution of suburban school funding to urban schools. Obama cannot achieve this last and most controversial redistributive goal without first gaining control of the day-to-day business of American schooling, what your children learn. So he has systematically set about creating a national curriculum for America's schools very arguably in violation of both the Constitution and the law.

While the public language of Obama's education policy is "standards, standards, standards," the actual plan is "federal control, federal control, federal control." Obama's hidden goal is to lower standards by pushing a weak curriculum and soft tests on the states. High standards are an obstacle to Obama's real aim of economic redistribution. In the eyes of education leftists like Obama, high standards make it harder for poor and minority children to get into good colleges. The truth is that high education standards, properly taught, lift everyone up, with arguably greater benefits going to poor and minority students. Unfortunately, the education left is looking for shortcuts to a forced equality. In its eyes, gutting standards is the easiest way to stop some children from doing better than others.

Look carefully at Obama's ambitious plans for a national education standards, and you will find hidden beneath it a still bolder plan to fund urban school districts with suburban money. Ultimately Obama would like to effectively merge urban and suburban school systems, a goal that can be reached through a combination of student transfers across district lines and assorted redistributive tax schemes. Technically, the national government has no power to mandate any of this. Yet a series of regulatory carrots and sticks imposed on pain of losing federal funding has the potential to move the nation's urban and suburban school systems toward effective merger. The same technique has already gone surprisingly far toward imposing a national school curriculum, in apparent defiance of the Constitution and the law.

So let us first follow the trail of Obama's stealthy efforts to create a national education curriculum, after which we can find an even bigger prize, the route from a national curriculum to a plan to redistribute suburban school funding to the cities.

A BILL AYERS LEGACY

The confluence of Obama's education reforms with the regional equity movement is yet another chapter in the story of the president's deep ties to political radicals. In this case, in addition to Obama's years of education work with the unrepentant Weather Underground terrorist Bill Ayers, the key figure is Linda Darling-Hammond, an influential proponent of a politicized curriculum. When it comes to education issues, Ayers and Darling-Hammond are very much on the same page.

The president does not personally coordinate his education

policy with Bill Ayers in the way that he works on regionalism
with his old Gamaliel colleague Mike Kruglik. How could
Obama invite Ayers to the Oval Office after the explosive 2008
controversy over his political ties to the former domestic terrorist
and Weather Underground leader? Yet his alliance with Ayers
does predict the direction of Obama's education policies.

Barack Obama and Bill Ayers worked together from 1999 to
2002 as board members of the left-leaning Woods Fund of Chicago.[1] Obama played a substantial role in placing Ayers on the
board, all of which was part of a broader Obama-led strategy to
increase Woods Fund support for community organizing. Along
with channeling grant money to radical groups like ACORN and
the Midwest Academy, Obama and Ayers directed substantial
funding to Gamaliel's regionalist crusade.[2]

Obama and Ayers also jointly ran an education foundation
called the Chicago Annenberg Challenge (CAC).[3] Obama's role
at CAC seems to have been to keep money flowing to radical
allies that he and Ayers shared, like ACORN and Gamaliel. Ayers,
who hated standardized tests, was much more interested in political indoctrination than in teaching basic skills. One of his projects was a "peace school," where kids celebrated milestones in the
history of the United Nations instead of traditional American
holidays. After giving out well over one hundred million dollars
to their community organizer buddies, Obama and Ayers had no
discernible improvement in educational performance to show for
it. In fact the determination that CAC had failed to improve test
scores in the low-performing schools it was trying to help was
made by the foundation's own evaluators.[4]

Obama's sojourn with Ayers on the hard left of the education
world may seem a far cry from the president's current education
policy. At first some open continuity with the Ayers years was a
real possibility because it looked for a while as though Obama

were going to appoint as secretary of education Bill Ayers's favorite education expert, the leftist Linda Darling-Hammond.[5] A leading Obama adviser during the presidential campaign and transition period, she is best known as a critic of traditional high-stakes tests who strongly favors "teaching for social justice"—that is, using everything from ideologically charged readings to politicized math problems to turn children into "progressive" activists. But Obama in the end passed over her in favor of Arne Duncan, who ostensibly backs demanding standards and tests. The administration's education policy now centers on efforts to craft a core curriculum, national standards, and systematic testing for the nation's schools. To a casual observer, the days of Obama's education partnership with the likes of Bill Ayers and Chicago's education hard left are a thing of the past.

But not really. Obama is deft at playing an outside game with the public but an inside game for himself. Darling-Hammond didn't become the secretary of education, but she has emerged instead as a key leader in the administration-orchestrated effort to create national standards and tests. That is to say, Obama has arranged for an enemy of traditional academic standards to police those standards. The result will be standards that aren't really standards at all.

Darling-Hammond's focus now, moreover, is an audacious new program for turning the administration's Common Core Initiative into a lever for a heavily redistributionist school-funding policy. That would be a great leap forward for the regional equity movement. Should Darling-Hammond's plan come fully into effect, the difference between urban and suburban school districts would effectively be erased, local control would be out, the federal government would be in charge of national education policy, and the federalist system as the founders envisioned it would be a long way closer to becoming a dead letter.

PIG IN A POKE

The Obama administration is well down the road to imposing a Common Core of standards on America's schools, with an accompanying curriculum and tests.[6] That might sound like a fairly conservative idea. Standards for everyone! And indeed, some conservatives have been fooled. Not everything that sounds like a standard is the genuine article, however. Obama hasn't told us exactly what the standards are going to be. He wants us to trust him. And anyway, with all the controversy over the economy, no one's been paying much attention to what's shaping up to be the biggest transformation of American schooling, maybe since the adoption of the Constitution.

The Constitution of course is silent on education. It leaves schooling up to the states. Throughout most of American history the federal government has played a minimal role in education. Locally controlled school districts and state governments were in charge instead. Since World War II, however, between the response to *Sputnik* and the establishment of the Department of Education as a cabinet-level agency, the federal role has increased. Still, the Constitution has continued to block federal control of the curriculum.

Obama's ambitious plan is to use a combination of federal power and taxpayer dollars to persuade the states to do "voluntarily" what the federal government cannot directly order them to do. Whether Obama's approach is constitutional remains to be seen. Yet this is Obama's strategy, and so far it's working.

To understand why the idea of a federally controlled school curriculum is worrisome, let's take a trip down memory lane. Back in the mid-1990s Lynne Cheney waged a pitched battle against liberal educators over left-leaning national history standards, whose initial development she herself had funded while serving as the chairwoman of the National Endowment for the Humanities. It's not unusual for conservatives to get burned when the money they give to improve education gets hijacked by leftist ideologues, as Cheney's grant was by a group of UCLA historians obsessed by race, class, and gender. Something similar happened to Walter Annenberg, the wealthy conservative donor who ended up funding the education foundation run by Bill Ayers and Barack Obama. But when Lynne Cheney had a good look at the history standards she'd commissioned, she put her foot down. The new curriculum played American history as a never-ending story of oppression. Cheney fought back, and the new history standards were eventually dropped when even many Democratic lawmakers turned against them.[7]

Americans need to remember that fiasco—the hijacking by leftists of a well-meaning attempt to nationalize education—before they sign on to a national standards project again. But the real problem is that President Obama and the education left also remember the history standards battle. So now they're too smart to actually say what America's new education curriculum is going to be. Instead they're trying to get all the states to sign off on the unprecedented idea of a national curriculum, sight unseen. By the time the actual standards come out, Obama hopes it will be too late for the states to back out of their commitment. And of course, by the time the actual content of our new national curriculum is revealed, Obama will quite possibly have been re-elected. You might think that states accustomed to controlling their own education standards, many of them run by Republicans, would have refused to sign off on the Obama administration's curricular pig in a poke. Yet so far well over forty states have jumped on the bandwagon. How was this possible, and where is Obama really taking us with this project?

AGAINST JOHN WAYNE

Suppose that in a major public address Barack Obama were to say the following: "My fellow Americans, to be honest, I have some serious reservations about the way this country is structured. In America we have this strong bias toward individual action. You know, we idolize the John Wayne hero who comes in to correct things with both guns blazing. But individual actions, individual dreams are not sufficient. We must unite in collective action, build collective institutions and organizations. Locally those collective actions and institutions have got to be pitched at the regional level in such a way as to unite small towns and suburbs with nearby cities. The whole federalist system, as the founders created it, is far too geared toward John Wayne–style individualism. You pick up and move to a suburb in search of your American dream. But that leaves less well-off folks behind, so classic federalism extracts a price this country can no longer afford to pay. The only way to make certain this nation's wealth gets more equally divided among all Americans is to run our country more centrally. That way no one can pick up and take his tax money to another town, suburb, or state without sharing it with someone less fortunate. That's why I plan to do everything in my power to advance federal and regional control of America's tax money and especially of America's system of education, so as to eliminate the local differences upon which our long but troubled tradition of John Wayne–style individualism rests."

That speech would not go over well with the American public although I believe it is an accurate rendering of the thinking behind the president's policies. In fact I've taken several lines at the beginning of this imaginary speech from an interview Obama gave to a Chicago paper when he first ran for public office in

1995.[8] (The portion from "In America we have this strong bias" to "build collective institutions and organizations" is a direct quote from Obama.)

So if you're President Obama and this is what you believe, how do you advance such an unpopular agenda in the area of education without alienating voters prior to your reelection campaign? Above all, you proceed in such a way as to discourage public debate. Here is a guide.

Step 1: Instead of asking Congress to appropriate money in support of your new education policy, thereby provoking public discussion of the issue, insert the funding for your key education initiative in a massive stimulus package, passed rapidly and with virtually no debate even on economic policy, much less education. That is precisely how President Obama procured the $4.35 billion, to be used solely at the Department of Education's discretion, for his Race to the Top Initiative. From the start Race to the Top was a kind of end run around the conventional legislative process. Writing in 2011 for Washington's insider paper *The Hill*, the education expert Jane Robbins made the point: "The Race to the Top program has been tinged with subterfuge from the beginning."[9]

Step 2: Now that you've got a huge pile of money free from congressional constraints and even public debate, use it as a lure to move the country's education system toward a federally controlled curriculum. Make the willingness to adopt a national Common Core a virtual condition of receiving Race to the Top grants, even before the standards and curriculum are finalized.

Now things get tricky. Technically a federally designed curriculum for the nation's schools would be both illegal and unconstitutional. The Tenth Amendment to the Constitution reserves control over education to the states and the people. Not only that, but the Elementary and Secondary Education Act, the U.S. Department of Education's 1979 enabling legislation and even the No Child Left Behind Act of 2001 all forbid the creation of either national education standards or a national curriculum.[10] So how do you get around all this?

Step 3: Orchestrate the creation of a national curriculum and standards from the White House while denying central control. Recruit publicly unaccountable groups like the National Governors Association to sponsor the project. Bring in the massively wealthy Gates Foundation for funding and supervision.[11] See to it that your former education adviser Linda Darling-Hammond (too controversial to be appointed secretary of education) is the leading presence at one of the private groups actually designing the curriculum and standards. And voilà! You, the president, have just used a combination of stealth, fancy legislative footwork, and the lure of big money in tough economic times to effectively circumvent both the Constitution and the law. Congratulations!

By acting without proper public debate, withholding details of the standards, testing regime, and curriculum he is pushing, and threatening to withhold federal funding from states that refuse to jump on the national standards bandwagon, Obama is making cash-strapped states an offer they can't refuse. Technically the states are "voluntarily" buying into this national Common Core idea. In fact they are selling their constitutional birthright for a mess of pottage, as Obama lays the foundations of an unprecedented federalization of America's schools. And all that is only part one of the plan.

A number of observers have remarked on the stealthy nature of President Obama's Common Core Initiative.[12] Here, for example, is the University of Arkansas professor and education blogger Jay Greene, commenting on the advocates of a national curriculum:

> . . . their entire project depends on stealth. If we
> have an open and vigorous debate about whether it is
> desirable for our large, diverse country to have

a uniform national set of standards, curriculum, and assessments, I am confident that they would lose. . . . I continue to believe that the chief architects of the nationalization campaign at the Gates Foundation and the U.S. Department of Education are intentionally concealing the full extent of their nationalization effort to improve its political prospects. For example, repeatedly describing the effort as "voluntary" and led by the states is obviously false and misleading, especially as the primary impetus was financial rewards during Race to the Top. . . .[13]

Greene is right to say that were they presented openly and honestly, Americans would reject Obama's plans to nationalize the country's education system. The framers of the Constitution understood perfectly well that the education of children ought to be governed by their parents, families, and neighbors.[14] Americans enthusiastically embrace this responsibility by holding local school officials responsible for their decisions. But how will parents be able to give a piece of their mind to some anonymous Washington education bureaucrat, much less an employee of a the Gates Foundation or an adviser to a private education consortium with a federal contract (like Linda Darling-Hammond) once these bodies have seized effective control of the nation's schools?[15]

NO GOLD STANDARD

Why exactly does President Obama want to take all this trouble to impose a national curriculum, education standards, and a system of testing on America's schools? Believe it or not, he is doing it because he's hostile to the whole idea of standards and testing. Tests and standards separate students out on the basis of achievement. The education left opposes that sort of ranking because it reveals "disparities." Racial and ethnic minorities as well as low-income students often do less well on standardized tests than do the children of the middle class. The right way to correct for that of course is to improve the ability of all students to meet high standards. The education left, however, prefers a shortcut to a false equality. It hopes to trash real education standards, so as to pretend that differences in achievement don't exist. That way low-performing poor and minority students will find it easier to get into college whether they're truly prepared or not. Differences in college admissions between urban and suburban students will begin to equalize, not because of genuine parity but through the suppression of real measures of educational achievement.

Sure enough, the limited information we have about the still undefined and incomplete Common Core being orchestrated by the Obama administration tells us that it will lower standards rather than raise them. Says Andrew Porter, the dean of the University of Pennsylvania School of Education: "Our research shows that the common-core standards do not represent a meaningful improvement over existing state standards. . . . The common core is not a new gold standard—it's firmly in the middle of the pack of current curricula."[16] Ze'ev Wurman, a mathematics, engineering, and science expert and a member of California's commission reviewing the Common Core, says: "This framework simply teaches our students science appreciation, rather than science."[17] And this is before we've seen the Common Core's testing system, which is even now being designed by the nation's leading opponents of standardized tests. An already mediocre core curriculum will surely be dumbed down still further by a weak testing program.[18]

It's particularly disheartening to see the hugely successful education reforms undertaken by Massachusetts cast aside by that state's adoption of Obama's Common Core. Under Republican governor William Weld, Massachusetts adopted rigorous standards, with a heavy emphasis on classic literature and academic content. Over the past fifteen or so years, Massachusetts has risen from being a middling performer on national tests to a consistently top-ranked state. In 2005 it became the first state ever to finish first in every one of the four categories measured by the National Assessment of Educational Progress (often called Americans' report card). Massachusetts students swept every category again in 2007 and 2009.[19]

Poor and minority students have not been passed over by this progress. Performance gaps keyed to race and income have actually narrowed in Massachusetts. In fact scores for African Americans and Hispanics have been rising more quickly than those of white students. In 2008 E. D. Hirsch, an expert on educational standards, said, "If you are a disadvantaged parent with a school-age child, Massachusetts is . . . the state to move to."[20]

You'd think the Massachusetts experience would serve as a model for the rest of the country, maybe especially for those on the political left. Yet the temptation to gut educational standards instead of doing the hard work it takes to meet them is too great. Massachusetts governor Deval Patrick has thrown over his own state's successful education experiment in favor of the untried, untested, undefined, but sure-to-be-dumbed-down, national core curriculum being pushed by his close political ally Barack Obama.

AYERS AND DARLING-HAMMOND

The key to Obama's second term education plans lies in the role being played in the administration-orchestrated Common Core program by Linda Darling-Hammond. Darling-Hammond was

Obama's education adviser during campaign 2008 and led his postelection transition team. She was on the fast lane to appointment as secretary of education until her leftism alienated even many Democrats.[21]

Shortly after Darling-Hammond was passed over for education secretary in favor of Arne Duncan, Bill Ayers himself came out with a column on the issue at the Huffington Post. If it were up to him, said Ayers, he would have picked Darling-Hammond for the job: ". . . then again I would have picked Noam Chomsky for [S]tate . . . Bernardine Dohrn for Attorney General . . . Paul Krugman for [T]reasury, and Amy Goodman for Press Secretary."[22] Yet Ayers admitted that the attacks on Darling-Hammond had destroyed her potential effectiveness as a cabinet member. He ended the piece by railing against standardized tests and advocating a redistribution of resources to the poor and minorities as a payment on America's "educational debt" (a popular variation on the reparations idea supported by Darling-Hammond as well as him).[23] Along with a politicized curriculum (another Ayers specialty), those are the key goals of the education left. As it turns out, Darling-Hammond may now be in a better position to gut standards, redistribute money, and politicize the curriculum than if she'd become a heavily scrutinized and controversial secretary of education.

The Ayers–Darling-Hammond link is no fluke. Both were leaders of the small schools movement, which was supposedly about reducing school size but was in fact about creating places to push leftist politics, like the peace school.[24] Ayers and Darling-Hammond have also worked together. She contributed to a collection of essays edited and published by Ayers in 1998 (when Ayers and Obama were working together at their own education foundation in Chicago). Darling-Hammond's contribution to that volume emphasized funding disparities between urban and suburban schools and praised the nonstandardized alternative assessments (like having students keep personal journals instead of taking tests) popular in the experimental schools that sprouted up in the 1960s.[25]

Like Ayers, Darling-Hammond has even edited her own volume of essays on teaching for "social justice."[26] Her writings on the topic would not sit well with most Americans. She appears to like making what she calls "[w]hite, middle class, heterosexual" students and teachers squirm.[27] She seems happiest when she gets her guilty targets apologizing for their "unspoken privileges."[28]

But Darling-Hammond doesn't just attack "sexuality, race, and gender privilege."[29] Her other favorite target is the insularity of "[w]hite, middle-class, suburban America."[30] Darling-Hammond is always looking for a way to guarantee "equity" between suburban and urban schools.[31] Nothing bothers her more than America's practice of funding schools from local taxes.[32] In effect her ideal curriculum could serve as a kind of propaganda arm for the regional equity movement.

It's clear from Darling-Hammond's writings that her long-term goal is to circumvent America's localized governance structures by centrally funding and administering the nation's schools, on the European model.[33] Just as the regional equity movement's strategy is to increase the reach of regional governing bodies before actually proposing tax sharing, so Darling-Hammond hopes that laying down a national curriculum will set a precedent for greater federal control of America's education system, even in matters of funding.

TAKE ME TO YOUR LEADER

What exactly is Darling-Hammond's role in shaping the new Common Core? Two major consortia are now devising a set of tests to measure mastery of the Core's education standards.

Between them they are splitting $360 million in federal Race to the Top money, $176 million of which goes to Darling-Hammond's group.[34] One knowledgeable teacher quoted in *Education Week* describes what's coming as "a huge departure from the kinds of tests most kids currently take."[35] That's not surprising, since Darling-Hammond is a prominent critic of standardized tests and a fan of far fuzzier "alternative" measurement instead.

Darling-Hammond is the leading presence at the Smarter Balanced Assessment Consortium, whose actual testing plans remain disturbingly undefined. The tests themselves will be ready only sometime in 2014 and 2015, conveniently several years into a possible second Obama term.[36] The Smarter Consortium was formed through the consolidation of several smaller groups. That consolidation apparently came in response to the Obama administration's decision to award money to only a very few applicants. This move had the effect of putting Darling-Hammond in charge of the huge chunk of the assessment pie.[37]

Although Darling-Hammond doesn't formally lead the Smarter Balanced Assessment Consortium, education experts generally treat her as the group's leading figure.[38] Perhaps mindful of the controversy surrounding her far-left views, she seems intent on downplaying her role. When *Education Week* reported that the Smarter group was "under the leadership" of Darling-Hammond, she contacted the paper to deny it, claiming to be just one of many people advising the consortium, which was itself supposedly being led by state chiefs and assessment leaders from the states.[39]

That denial is unconvincing. We've seen that state "leadership" of the Common Core is actually more like state followership of the federal money being dangled, with heavy conditions, by the Obama administration. And here's how the newsletter of the Smarter Balanced Assessment Consortium described

Darling-Hammond's role in November 2011: "Throughout the summer, Dr. Linda Darling-Hammond, the Consortium's Senior Research Advisor . . . led the development of the content specifications [of the tests] in collaboration with experts in the field."[40] Clearly, Darling-Hammond is leading the actual development of testing by the Smarter Balanced Assessment Consortium, which in turn now controls about half the national testing franchise.

So by limiting the number of competitive grants, the Obama administration has created a situation in which the president's former education adviser, who is the top national opponent of standardized tests, is now effectively in charge of designing tests for half the country. Yet the broader public has virtually no idea that any of this is happening.

A TROUBLING VISION

Gutting America's educational testing standards is only the beginning of what Darling-Hammond has in mind. In January 2012 Darling-Hammond published a piece in the leftist *Nation* magazine, pointing toward her broader goals for the Common Core.[41] Like Obama's regionalist mentors, Darling-Hammond compares America's education system with South African apartheid. She also suggests that a real solution to the problem of poverty would require government to guarantee "housing, healthcare, and basic income security" to all. She then attacks standardized tests and praises nations that centrally control their schools.

Yet the real novelty in this piece is Darling-Hammond's call to create common resource standards that would work on the model of the new Common Core standards. She wants to use these common resource standards to make the receipt of federal education money conditional on the equalization of school funding across municipal lines.

The plan is sketched out in the 2020 Vision Roadmap, a document that Darling-Hammond helped put together and that she touts at the end of her *Nation* article.[42] The 2020 Vision Roadmap is filled with prescriptions for using federal carrots and sticks to force the sort of antisuburban reforms advocated by the regional equity movement. Consider the following passage: "The federal government should compel states to review inter- and intra-[school] district resource distribution using established indicators. States that fail to comply would be subject to withdrawal of federal funds, and the federal government would have the right to apply the direct remedy to correct the problem."[43] This would empower the federal government to negate America's local school funding system and force the redistribution of local tax money across municipal lines. The 2020 Vision Roadmap also proposes allowing students to transfer across school district lines, with transportation provided at government expense.[44]

Just as the combination of regional tax base sharing, growth boundaries, and low-income housing quotas supported by the regional equity movement would effectively abolish the suburbs, so Darling-Hammond's proposals would have the effect of eliminating distinctions between urban and suburban school districts in a given region. The combination of government-imposed revenue redistribution and government-funded cross–school district transfers would, in practical terms, mean the swallowing up of suburban school districts by nearby cities.

It could be argued that the Obama administration will stop at the Common Core. Just because Darling-Hammond wants common resource standards added to the Common Core doesn't mean that Obama will do as she asks. Voters would be fools to believe that, however. Given the fact that Darling-Hammond is now effectively steering the administration's most important education policy initiative, her outsize influence will surely continue. We've already learned that the president's Sustainable

Communities Initiative is being shaped behind the scenes by his former organizing mentor Mike Kruglik.[45] Obama's urban and regional policy has already been infused with equity standards crafted by his old leftist colleagues. We should therefore expect him to grant Darling-Hammond and her leftist colleagues the ability to craft a parallel educational equity agenda in a second term. In fact Darling-Hammond has already been appointed to the Obama administration's Department of Education Equity and Excellence Commission, which is charged with recommending "ways to restructure school finance systems to achieve equity in the distribution of educational resources and further student achievement and attainment."[46]

ENDGAME

The outlines of a revolutionary and profoundly redistributionist transformation of the way Americans live and govern themselves are now visible—to those who have eyes to see. The foundation has already been laid. If Obama can graft Darling-Hammond's common resource standards onto his common curricular standards and enforce them by regulation, on pain of loss of federal funding, he could force a gradual merger of urban and suburban school districts.

The country is in for some major surprises during a possible Obama second term. If it seems unlikely that a combination of federal carrots and sticks could usurp America's system of state and local school control, consider that we are already vastly closer to having an arguably illegal and unconstitutional national school curriculum than many would have thought possible. That was achieved through the powers of the presidency, a willingness to make an end run around the usual legislative process, and the lure of federal money in tough economic times. Having gotten this far toward fulfilling the redistributive goals that he and his hard-left colleagues have cherished for years, for the most part without the public even noticing, a reelected Obama will surely press the plan forward.

Once Obama begins to force a redistribution of suburban school funding to the cities, a central plank in his program to abolish the suburbs will be in place. A core reason for moving to the suburbs will slowly be rendered pointless, undercutting the engine of our prosperity and ending the American tradition of local control over schools. In the meantime those who saved and sacrificed for years to move to the suburbs will see their plans undermined, as the schools that drew them to new homes slowly lose their distinctive quality. Forced equality through redistribution will trump liberty, prosperity, and self-rule. Welcome to Obama's new America.

It doesn't stop there. Once we pull Obama's regionalist crusade out from its dusty hiding place, examine it, and grasp its tremendous personal importance for the president, a whole panoply of administration policies begins to make sense as part of a much larger effort to force redistribution from the suburbs to the cities. We've just seen this for education policy, and the implications go further still. Even Obama's signature issues, like health care reform and the stimulus package, take on new meaning once you recognize that the antisuburban redistributionist crusade has been the president's guiding light all along. So let's go big, with a panoramic view of Obama's first term in light of all that we've learned to date.

CHAPTER EIGHT

OBAMA IN A NEW LIGHT

Once you realize that President Obama supports his old mentor's efforts to abolish the suburbs, and has done so for years, virtually all his policies appear in a new light. Since this is where the president's heart lies, the regional equity crusade leads us straight to Obama's broader vision for America. Everything from his health care reform to the stimulus to regulatory decisions to his defense and foreign policies comes into better focus when illuminated by the regionalist sun.

Obama's effort to redistribute money from the suburbs to the cities is more than just a little-known but very important aspect of his policies. Taking from the suburbs to give to the cities is his main goal. True, he has never announced an overarching rationale for his administration's actions, much less admitted redistribution of suburban money as a major objective. Yet when we combine what Obama's memoir tells us about his core beliefs with knowledge of his Alinskyite political background and a broad consideration of his current policies, redistributing tax money to the cities emerges as the connecting thread.

A three-pronged approach will uncover the rationale behind

the Obama administration's actions. First, we'll explore the big-picture strategy offered by one of the regional equity movement's leading lights, which closely predicts the Obama administration's actions on a number of fronts. Second, analyzing the response of Obama and his allies to the Occupy Wall Street movement will tell us much about where Obama is going and how he has come so far in his first term. Finally, the slowly unfolding crisis of the European Union turns out to repeat and anticipate the dynamics of America's regional equity movement. Obama's attitude toward the postnational project exemplified by the European Union explains, and is explained by, his regionalist sympathies. Put them all together, and the big ideas behind the Obama administration's policies emerge from obscurity.

PETER DREIER

You can see the central rationale of the Obama administration's policies laid out in the writings of Peter Dreier, the E. P. Clapp Distinguished Professor of Politics at Occidental College. Dreier, a major figure in the regional equity movement, is a highly influential theorist of American socialism, community organizing, and urban politics.[1] He also advised Obama's 2008 presidential campaign.[2] Dreier is so deeply a part of the world that shaped Obama that it is well worth reviewing his background.

When Dreier was in junior high school, he heard a talk by Michael Harrington, the leading American socialist of the day. It was a life-changing moment. Harrington became first Dreier's hero, then his mentor, and eventually (when Dreier served on the national board of Harrington's group, the Democratic Socialists of America) Dreier's friend. One of Dreier's children is named in honor of Harrington.[3]

Dreier had been a journalism major at Syracuse University, an assistant professor of sociology at Tufts, and the lead organizer with the Massachusetts Tenants Organization when he joined the administration of the newly elected Boston mayor Ray Flynn in 1984.[4] Just before that, Dreier had produced a programmatic statement on Boston politics for Harrington's Democratic Socialists of America.

Dreier quickly became part of a small group of very left-leaning Flynn advisers nicknamed the Sandinistas. He pushed for heavily redistributive policies, many of which were blocked by Boston's city council. You would think that a prominent socialist like Dreier might be immune to attacks from the left, yet his policies did draw criticism from leftists for being too gradualist. Dreier also pushed for Flynn to support community groups like ACORN, which were just then beginning to use the federal Community Reinvestment Act to pressure banks into making subprime loans. Years later Dreier became one of ACORN's most prominent public supporters and defenders.

In 1983, just before he joined the Flynn administration, Dreier convened a panel at a conference sponsored by the Democratic Socialists of America. The panel was about community organizing and its links to socialism and electoral politics. A young Barack Obama, then a senior at Columbia University, attended that conference and shortly thereafter settled on community organizing as his vocation.[5] In general anyone interested in community organizing in the 1980s would have run into Dreier's writings.

Dreier believed that community organizations should serve as what he called socialist incubators, gradually pushing America toward redistributive policies, like a Canadian-style government-run health care system.[6] I tell the story of Dreier's influence on Obama's political world in my biography of the president, *Radical-in-Chief.*

After Flynn's mayoralty ended in 1993, Dreier became a professor at Occidental College. (This was well after Obama had departed Occidental for Columbia University.) Already a prominent theorist of socialism, community organizing, and urban affairs, Dreier was caught up in the regionalist movement in the mid-1990s, the same time that the Gamaliel Foundation in Chicago signed on to the regionalist agenda, with Obama's financial support. In 2000 Dreier and two coauthors, John Mollenkopf and Todd Swanstrom, published *Place Matters: Metropolitics for the Twenty-first Century.*[7] Along with the writings of David Rusk and Myron Orfield, Dreier's *Place Matters* is one of the most influential statements of the regionalist case.

In 2002 Dreier's life came full circle when *Place Matters* was given the Michael Harrington Book Award by a left-leaning subdivision of the American Political Science Association.[8] The Harrington Award goes to the "outstanding book that demonstrates how scholarship can be used in the struggle for a better world." *Place Matters* is best known for providing the Democrats with a strategy for splitting the suburbs, so as to create a new national majority for a platform of economic redistribution.[9]

DREIER'S PLAN

As noted, Dreier was an adviser to Obama's 2008 campaign, so the president clearly knows and values his work. In addition to systematically putting the case for regionalism, Dreier has sketched out a program for a comprehensive yet unobtrusive approach to urban policy. His vision bears an uncanny resemblance to the overall direction of Obama's presidency. Although Dreier has published many articles on urban issues, his book *Place Matters* and a 1996 article titled "The Struggle for Our Cities" are particularly useful for piecing together his views and then comparing them to the direction of the Obama administration.[10]

Dreier is a key figure in the world of community organizing, and as such he draws on the Alinskyite tradition of stealthy and pragmatic incrementalism in the service of a hard-left agenda. After making his case for the effective abolition of the suburbs, Dreier concludes, "Our perspective is at once radical and incremental."[11] This not only fits Alinsky's method but matches Michael Harrington's as well. Dreier says he modeled the politics advocated in *Place Matters* on Harrington's conception of a pragmatic socialism, or what Harrington called the "left wing of the possible."[12] It will take decades, says Dreier, to fulfill the regionalist agenda, meaning that he is willing to accept baby steps in the present.[13]

For example, Dreier suggests that the federal government should require that its various domestic programs be administered by regional bodies.[14] That such regional authorities might at first have little formal power does not concern him. The idea is to get regional governing bodies up and running with federal inducements, then to transfer authority from local governments to regional megacouncils over time.[15] We've seen that the Obama administration is taking exactly this course, structuring efforts on housing, transportation, jobs, and land use to be run by regional planning consortia. This is particularly so with the Sustainable Communities Initiative, but the regionalist impulse has also shaped administration projects like Energy Innovation Hubs and Regional Innovation Clusters. Regionalists continue to press the administration to travel much farther along these lines.[16] The danger is that once safely into his second term, Obama will do exactly that.

Dreier also wants to give unions and community organizations a substantial role within these regional authorities, which Obama's partnership with Kruglik's Building One America is ideally suited to do.[17] All this fits in nicely with Dreier's original vision from the 1980s of a socialism driven "from below" by leftist community organizations.[18] Harrington embraced this transformed view of socialism, rejecting the classic demand for the immediate nationalization of the means of production and replacing it instead with a gradualist program built from the ground up through community organizing and grassroots union activism. The idea was that leftist community organizations and unions should be granted a role on various public boards and authorities, thereby powering a national redistributionist agenda.[19]

Of course you don't have to be a socialist to favor the regionalist agenda. On the other hand, it helps. From Dreier's perspective, regionalist redistribution would appear to be a pragmatic way to advance socialism in the here and now. Dreier of course is an enthusiastic advocate of Myron Orfield's redistributive regional tax base sharing scheme, which the Obama administration's alliance with Building One America is designed to promote.[20]

Dreier sees stealth as fundamental to enacting the regionalist agenda, chiefly because our majority-suburban country would reject a city-centric redistributionist agenda were it presented openly. Dreier praises regionalist programs that proceed "below the political radar screen."[21] He also favors deploying regionalist arguments focused not only on "equity" but on "efficiency and the environment" although redistribution would appear to be his overwhelming concern.[22] We've seen this sort of obfuscation praised by other equity-focused regionalists for creating "an optimal level of fog." Regional equity advocates are just as happy to achieve their redistributionist aims "through the back door" as by open advocacy. In keeping with this, Dreier suggests that redistributionist measures ought to be "unobtrusive, and just one part of a larger package . . ."[23]

CITIES IN HIDING

That brings us to the Obama administration's signature policies: health care reform and the stimulus. Neither has been billed as a way of redistributing money to cities. Yet Dreier effectively treats both policies as exactly that. In 1996 Dreier suggested that national health insurance would be a far more politically sellable way to channel aid to the cities than federal grants explicitly targeted to urban areas.[24] Four years later, in *Place Matters*, Dreier again recommended universal health insurance as an essential part of any redistributionist city-centered agenda. The idea is that government-guaranteed health care will benefit the urban poor most of all, effectively hiding a redistributionist policy for the cities within a larger package.[25]

For those who suspect that Obamacare is meant to turn by degrees into a flat-out socialist single-payer system, Dreier's work shows that someone who holds the president's ear really does advocate a stealthy and incremental radicalism geared toward socialist aims. Obama's disinclination to insist upon the open and immediate creation of a health care public option, by the way, no more disproves the president's radicalism than did Dreier's impatient critics on the left disprove his socialism.

Dreier's 1996 article "The Struggle for Our Cities" also pushes "public works and infrastructure grants" as another unobtrusive way to channel money from the rest of the country toward the cities.[26] The federal stimulus bill was focused of course on public works and infrastructure grants. These grants may not have gone exclusively to the cities, yet Dreier's point is that because cities have loads of concentrated infrastructure, this kind of spending disproportionately benefits them and is politically much easier to sell than direct urban aid. Once general infrastructure spending is approved, moreover, an administration so inclined can always channel the money disproportionately to cities without much notice's being taken. And of course Michelle Obama's "Shhhh!" confirmed that the stimulus disguised a series of controversial War on Poverty–style programs, passed without proper public debate.

We've already learned that Obama larded the stimulus with education expenditures that by rights ought to have gone through a separate congressional debate. The Race to the Top program, folded within the stimulus, turned out to be a stealthy way of imposing a low-quality, left-biased national curriculum on the nation's schools, very arguably in defiance of the Constitution and the law.

And sure enough, Dreier recommends creating a set of national standards geared to inner-city schools, combined with federal moves that would require states to equalize education spending across distinct districts.[27] In his words, "radical measures are clearly in order."[28] So Dreier's comprehensive program to channel money to the cities would appear to have predicted the Obama administration's redistributionist and antisuburban education policy very nicely, including the call for such programs to remain "unobtrusive" and "just one part of a larger package," in this case the stimulus package.

TRAPPED

Dreier's socialist inclinations don't stop at redistribution. He recognizes that redistributive policies can never succeed unless the government limits freedom of movement, what Dreier calls capital mobility.[29] So long as businesses and individuals can pick up and move, they have the means to escape onerous taxation. This freedom of movement, central to our liberties, is the bane of leftists like Dreier.

Dreier explains that every time community organizers ask a city to adopt redistributive programs, they're attacked for stifling the economy and undercutting business. As he puts it, "Progressive redistributive policies hurt cities because they entail increased taxes and/or reduced services for those residents and businesses that contribute most to the city's tax base and economic well-being."[30] The solution, suggests Dreier, is to undercut freedom of movement—that is, to fetter capital mobility. If companies are trapped, unable to move, they and their employees will have no choice but to submit to a given city's redistributive tax and spending plans. Blocking the mobility of capital can succeed only at the national level, adds Dreier, because it requires an authority capable of controlling movement between cities and states.

Here is where Dreier's backing for the notorious community group ACORN comes in. ACORN's platform long included a series of measures designed to inhibit the free movement of businesses. It wanted companies seeking to relocate to apply for what it called exit visas. In ACORN's vision, the power to grant those visas for business moves within the United States would be held by community boards—with strong representation from groups like ACORN, of course.[31] These proposals, long supported by Dreier, have been called by the Manhattan Institute scholar Sol Stern, undisguised authoritarian socialism.[32] Stern also notes that requiring wealthy or middle-class individuals to obtain exit visas before moving from a city to a suburb would be the logical next step.

The action taken by the Obama-controlled National Labor Relations Board (NLRB) to block Boeing's planned move from the state of Washington to South Carolina is an excellent example of an attack on capital mobility.[33] The NLRB claimed that Boeing's decision to transfer a second production line for its new 787 Dreamliner plane was an illegal attempt to discourage labor strikes. Yet even the liberal *New York Times* noted that companies had long moved plants to nonunion states, adding: "It is highly unusual for the federal government to seek to reverse a corporate decision as important as the location of a plant." John Judis, of the liberal *New Republic*, said this step by the NLRB might be "the most radical thing the Obama administration has done."[34]

While the NLRB withdrew its lawsuit against Boeing's investment in South Carolina in late 2011, this happened only after Boeing had effectively capitulated to the Obama administration and its union partners by paring back on its relocation. The *Wall Street Journal* noted in an editorial that the NLRB's shot across the bow had significantly degraded the ability of companies to freely move around the country.[35]

We learned in chapter 5 that in his memoir, *Dreams from My Father*, Obama mourned his inability to get manufacturers to relocate from the suburbs to the cities. Like Dreier, Obama sees the issue of capital mobility through a city-centric lens. This stance by the Obama-controlled NLRB, called radical even by the *New Republic*, will likely be further entrenched as policy should Obama be reelected. Once again, Dreier's comprehensive plan for the cities has predicted an important Obama administration move.

Dreier also advocates major cuts in defense spending to help pay for the cities, along with reforms to make labor organizing easier.[36] President Obama of course has proposed major defense cuts to help pay for his domestic programs, along with card check legislation that would eliminate the secret ballot in votes on unionization.

Obviously moves like defense cuts, card check, and health care reform can be advocated for reasons unconnected to urban policy. Generally, Dreier's ambitious and wide-ranging urban plan overlaps with actions supported by many on the left, for a wide variety of reasons.

REDISTRIBUTOR IN CHIEF

All that being granted, it is nonetheless of interest that a prominent theorist of community organizing and onetime adviser to Obama has put forward a comprehensive set of proposals geared toward redistributing money to America's cities, proposals that closely match Obama's actions. Dreier's plan supplies a possible systematic rationale for a wide variety of Obama administration policies. That rationale also fits exceedingly well with what we know of Obama's past experience and deepest commitments.

Obama may or may not have received Dreier's recommendations directly although it seems likely that he would have discussed his governing strategy with a onetime adviser known for offering such formulations. In any case, Dreier's plan captures the ethos of Obama's community organizing colleagues in the regionalist movement. At minimum it tells us how someone who comes from Obama's political world would go about governing. It helps explain Obama, whether the connection is indirect or direct. If we understand the president's policy agenda as a series of more and less obvious strategies for redistributing money to the cities, a great deal falls into place.

Obama makes a similar point himself in his book *The Audacity of Hope*. There, while he expresses support for programs directly targeted to the needs of minorities, he suggests that universal programs can achieve the same ends in a more politically acceptable fashion. He gives the following example: ". . . a plan for universal health-care coverage would do more to eliminate health disparities between whites and minorities than any race-specific programs we might design."[37] Obama didn't sell his health care reform as a redistributive plan. Yet he apparently thinks of it that way. The same is surely true for many of his other policies.

The claim that Obama strongly favors the redistribution of

wealth is not new. Critics have made the point ever since the "Joe the Plumber" incident during the 2008 campaign, when Obama said he wanted to "spread the wealth around" and the Republican nominee, John McCain, attacked the remark as socialist.[38] Obama has also grown more explicit of late about his plans to reduce income disparities while pretending that he's targeted the pocketbooks of only a few millionaires and billionaires.[39] In general, however, Obama has greatly underplayed the redistributive aspects of his policies. He certainly hasn't highlighted his support for a movement whose core aim is regional tax base sharing. Plans to equalize spending between urban and suburban school districts are likewise almost totally off the national radar screen.

To the extent that the cities receive a net redistributive gain from programs like health care reform and the infrastructure portions of the stimulus, wealth is being taken from rural areas as well as suburbs. It's Obama's scheme for regional tax base sharing, hatched in conjunction with his old community organizing buddies, that is specifically designed to take from the suburbs to pay for the cities. So both rural and suburban areas are under Obama's tax gun, but suburban areas especially so.

We already know that Obama condescends to rural folk who bitterly "cling" to their Bibles and guns.[40] His attitude toward the suburbs as expressed in his memoir, however, is a step closer to actively hostile. We've seen that Obama's organizing colleagues, with whom he still works, see the suburbs as execrable symbols of an "American apartheid." Given all this, it's likely that in Obama's mind the suburbs are the special targets of all his redistributive plans.

IS HE SOCIALIST?

Does Obama's support for regional tax base sharing and a whole panoply of other redistributive policies prove that he is a socialist?

At a minimum the evidence offered in this book significantly strengthens the case that he is a socialist. That a prominent theorist of socialism and community organizing like Peter Dreier has focused his efforts on regionalism also indicates that the movement is at the very least compatible with socialism. By that I mean not the Marxism of violent revolution but the sort of pragmatic and incremental democratic socialism embraced by both Saul Alinsky and Michael Harrington.

If you're already inclined to think that Barack Obama is a socialist, all that we've learned in this book can be taken as further proof. On the other hand, the question of Obama's precise ideological perspective is a separate issue. Resolving it requires a careful examination of the president's political history, from the past right through to the present.

For our purposes here it is in no way necessary to resolve the question of Obama's precise ideology. All we really need to know is that his support for a movement devoted to the spread of regional tax base sharing shows that his commitments are redistributive to a degree unprecedented for an American chief executive. Whether you want to call Obama's redistributive policies socialism, social democracy, or extreme liberalism, the point is that the president of the United States sits at the far-left end of the conventional American political spectrum.

OCCUPY WALL STREET

During his first two years in office, Obama offered few ideological justifications for his proposals, which he presented as pragmatic responses to America's economic problems. He did, however, take a number of class warfare swipes at targets like "fat cat bankers" and the Chamber of Commerce in the first half of his term.[41] This was designed to stir up a populist antibusiness movement of the left, the long-cherished goal of Obama's community organizing mentors. Like Peter Dreier, many of Obama's organizing colleagues were closely allied with Michael Harrington's Democratic Socialists of America. It was Harrington who first came up with what he called a party realignment strategy, which could be powered by a populist, antibusiness movement of the left.[42]

Harrington and his allies hoped to use a left-populist movement to drive business interests out of the Democratic Party into the Republican Party. That might seem counterproductive, yet the hope was that the movement's energy would draw poor, minority, and working-class voters into the Democratic Party in numbers sufficient to offset the loss of probusiness voters to the Republicans.

At that point the two parties would be polarized along class lines, a party of the haves versus a party of the have-nots. Harrington believed that once America's political parties were divided by class, the party of the have-nots—that is, the Democrats—would inevitably drift toward a more explicitly socialist platform. So Harrington worked to turn the Democratic Party slowly to the left, in the hope of provoking a polarizing class-based battle that would eventually push an avowedly socialist politics to the forefront.

In the third year of his presidency Obama began to step up his class warfare attacks on millionaires and billionaires in their "corporate jets."[43] Finally he helped inspire a populist antibusiness movement of the left. It's called Occupy Wall Street.

The rise of Occupy Wall Street is a be-careful-what-you-wish-for moment for Obama. By focusing on income inequality, the gap between the "wealthiest 1 percent" and everyone else, Occupy Wall Street advances Obama's redistributive goals. Traditionally Americans achieve prosperity by growing the economy for all, not by seizing and redistributing wealth. Occupy Wall

Street and Obama want to change all that. The problem for Obama is that Occupy Wall Street is far too open about its goals.

Obama the Alinskyite prefers to remain mum on his ultimate aims while transforming America into a heavily redistributive society through a slowly escalating series of concrete reforms. Many of Obama's steps are taken in stealth, as we've seen. Reversing all that, Occupy Wall Street speaks only of its ultimate goal, a world without income inequality, meaning the elimination of our current economic system. Gradual reform in the service of this radical goal is disdained by OWSers as a sellout. So Obama's got his populist, antibusiness movement of the left. Yet instead of turning to putty in the president's hands, a force he can quickly marshal in support of his incremental redistributionist reforms, Occupy Wall Street has shunned everyday politics. Worse, it threatens to give the game away by making Obama's radical aims too obvious too soon.

Obama has expressed sympathy for the frustrations that supposedly launched Occupy Wall Street and even picked up on its theme of the wealthiest 1 percent in his speech at Osawatomie, Kansas.[44] The president would love nothing more than to turn Occupy Wall Street into his strong right arm. Yet he worries that this strategy may fail, leaving him with the taint of the movement's radicalism, so he keeps some distance between him and the occupiers. The revealing point is that Obama and the Democrats didn't condemn this extremist movement from the start. Instead they've pumped it up, trying to ride it and guide it when they should have been running away.

DEMOCRATS ADRIFT

The Occupy Wall Street movement was launched by Kalle Lasn, the founder and editor of *Adbusters* magazine. Lasn and his anarchist followers hoped to start a revolution that would "kill capitalism."[45] These anarchists are the core organizers of the Occupy movement, and their aim is to eradicate not only capitalism but the state.[46] The occupiers won't publish a list of political demands because they want to abolish the government, not seize it. This anarchist position leads inevitably to attempts at violent overthrow, and even many occupiers who avoid violence support those who do engage in it. The movement has given us plenty of examples: stones hurled through bank windows; attempted building takeovers; actions designed to choke off the flow of capital by shutting down West Coast ports.[47] These aren't anomalies for the Occupy movement; they're the point.

The organizers who created Occupy Wall Street and dominate it still come from a collection of far-left parties and anarchist circles that have been demonstrating on the fringes of society since the violent protests against the World Trade Organization (WTO) in Seattle in 1999.[48] That history meant it was obvious from the start that this was an extremist movement, totally opposed to America's free enterprise system and willing to use violence to achieve its ends. Yet in hopes of turning the Occupy movement to their own purposes, Obama, his Democratic allies, and the media have largely averted their eyes from this reality.

The liberal editors of the *New Republic* are the exception that proves the rule. The magazine condemned the Occupy protests early on, correctly identifying the movement as radical and anti-capitalist.[49] Yet many, if not most, of the *New Republic*'s contributors broke with the editors and endorsed the Occupy movement, although it was transparently a continuation of the violent WTO protests that the magazine had condemned in a similar editorial more than a decade before.[50] The radicalism of the protesters hadn't changed since 1999, but the Democratic Party had. The Democrats and their allies in the media have simply lost the desire or the capacity to separate themselves from anticapitalist radicalism on the left.

This explains a lot about the media's decision to avert their eyes from Barack Obama's own radical past in 2008 and since. You can argue that the media's kid glove treatment of Obama's Alinskyite history is an effort to preserve the inspiring narrative of the first African American to ascend to the presidency. Yet that doesn't explain their refusal to face the truth about Occupy Wall Street. Race is not the issue here. We're looking instead at a leftward shift in the Democratic Party. This is what enabled a candidate as far to the left as Obama to secure the Democratic nomination for president in the first place.

THE RETURN OF BILL AYERS

We've already seen that Obama's long-standing alliance with Bill Ayers predicted the president's education policy. Obama and Ayers also worked together at the Woods Fund of Chicago to fund the regional equity movement, so important to the president's plans today. I've argued that the most important lesson of Obama's alliance with Ayers is the window it opens onto the broader network of Obama's leftist ties. Ayers's notoriety draws attention to a much larger issue: Obama's radical world. Everything we've learned in this book bears that out. Yet the seemingly narrower issue of Ayers's terrorist past turns out to have been important as well. His terrorist history, his refusal to repudiate it, Obama's tolerance for all that, and the media's lack of interest in the issue tell us a great deal about the Democratic Party's drift.

The symbol of Occupy Wall Street is the Guy Fawkes mask. Fawkes was a terrorist who tried to bring down the British government by blowing up Parliament during its opening ceremony.

That would have killed the king and the country's other leaders as well. Imagine blowing up the U.S. Capitol during a state of the union address. Fawkes was attempting something similar.[51]

The Fawkes mask was popularized by the 2006 film *V for Vendetta*, which glamorizes the anarchist sentiments that drive the occupiers today. The protesters might as well be wearing Bill Ayers masks because Fawkes is now a comparable symbol of domestic terrorism on the left. The occupiers have been advertising their violent, revolutionary plans on their faces. Yet the media will see no evil.

This is not a question of Obama, the Democrats, or the media's actually favoring violent terrorism. Yet the willingness of Chicago's liberals to accept and even to embrace Bill Ayers and Bernardine Dohrn, despite the pair's refusal to repudiate their violent past, was an early signal of a shift within the Democratic Party. Likewise, the media's refusal to probe the significance of Obama's deep and long-standing radical ties, with Ayers and many others, is of a piece with their willful blindness to the reality of the Occupy Wall Street movement. The Democrats have moved left, surrendering in the process their capacity either to recognize or to repudiate anticapitalist radicalism.

Obama's allies in the regional equity movement see America much the way the Occupy protesters do. The Gamaliel Foundation's 1999 regionalist manifesto excoriates America's wealthiest 1 percent, also identified as the "ruling classes," and plots a populist movement to overcome the 1 percent's supposed domination of the country. The difference is that Gamaliel follows the Alinskyite path, working gradually, through concrete reforms to achieve a redistributionist state. The occupiers, in contrast, want revolution now. Obama is smart enough to stick with the Alinskyite way. Yet he's not above making use of an openly hard-left populism, if he can get away with it without showing his cards too soon.

MORE THAN 1 PERCENT

With Obama expressing cautious support for the Occupy movement and escalating his class warfare assaults on millionaires and
billionaires, is his radicalism now on full display? Not yet. That's
why his support for Building One America's tax base sharing
scheme and Linda Darling-Hammond's plans to level funding
across urban and suburban school districts remain under the
public's radar.

Obama wants to entice Americans into supporting his redistributive plans in principle, with millionaires and billionaires as
his easy targets. Reelect him, and you'll quickly see that he is
after the pocketbooks of a whole lot more than just 1 percent of
us. His real target is America's middle class, suburbanites in particular. Many suburban voters now planning to support him will
find their incomes and their children's schools the targets of his
redistributive schemes in a second term. The 1 percent slogan is a
sham. If your income is in the top 50 percent, Obama is after you.

Families that make more than $250,000, subject to higher
taxes under Obama's current proposals, make up only 2.6 percent
of Americans.[52] The percentage that would be negatively affected
by regional tax base sharing and funding transfers away from suburban schools will be vastly higher. In *Why Obamacare Is Wrong
for America*, Grace-Marie Turner, James C. Capretta, Thomas P.
Miller, and Robert E. Moffit strip away the accounting gimmicks,
smoke and mirrors, and deceptive advertising Obama used to sell
health care reform and explain how the new law will inevitably
result in higher taxes on the middle class.[53] Obamacare's tricks
include taxes on medical companies bound to be passed on to
middle-class consumers, time delays on direct tax increases, and
the return of bracket creep (ended by the Reagan tax cuts). Since

the $200,000 threshold for individuals and the $250,000 threshold for couples paying higher Medicare taxes will not be indexed to inflation, normal inflation will gradually push large numbers of middle-class taxpayers into the higher tax category. The many forms of delayed and disguised tax increases built into Obamacare reveal the president's methods. He's saving his most controversial initiatives for a second term, including concerted moves to force regional tax base sharing on the states, and federal pressure to equalize urban and suburban school funding.

REDISTRIBUTION GOES GLOBAL

If you want to know where Obama is headed, look to Europe. This point is often made, yet it is particularly apt in the case of regionalism and in more ways than one. In the first place, leaders of the regional equity movement take Europe as their model. Linda Darling-Hammond wants America to copy Europe's centrally controlled education systems, john powell sees European social democracy as a cure for the supposedly egoistic American dream, and Bruce Katz lauds Europe for blazing the regionalist trail.[54] Regionalist redistribution and an end to local self-rule contradict everything Tocqueville found admirable about America and held up as a lesson for Europe. In effect Obama is running Tocqueville's project in reverse, slowly undercutting federalism and with it the characteristic American thirst for liberty that our constitutional system produces. Obama is doing it all, moreover, on the European model.

The centralized European social democratic state isn't the only template for regionalism, however. The postnational project of the European Union is a regionalist effort on a grand scale. It therefore tells us much about the foibles of Obama's plans for America.

Today Europe is in crisis. Its centralized and redistributive welfare states are collapsing from debt. These national debt crises in turn are being aggravated by the slow-motion attempt to create a European superstate out of a collection of separate countries. Gathering distinct economies and cultures under a single currency has pushed the Continent to the brink of disaster. Nations are unable to devalue or revalue their currencies as the situation demands. Wealthy nations subsidize weak ones yet reap hatred instead of gratitude as they effectively seize control of the economies and governments of their beneficiaries. European sovereignty and democracy are disappearing as bureaucrats in Brussels, unanswerable to voters, usurp control from national publics. It's not a pretty picture. Yet the crisis of the European project has much to tell us about Obama's aspirations for America and the world.

In a new book, *Sovereignty or Submission: Will Americans Rule Themselves or Be Ruled by Others?*, John Fonte sounds the alarm about the vastly underappreciated threat to American democracy posed by the global governance movement.[55] Fonte dissects this movement of international elites, which aims to place the sovereign decisions of democratic nation-states under the authority of bodies like the International Criminal Court and the United Nations. In effect the global governance movement wants to rope fiercely independent countries like the United States and Israel into a system controlled by the international, social democratic, European-based left. The idea is to use the United Nations to extend European norms until in practice they govern the West as a whole and eventually the globe itself. It's a long-term strategy for remaking the world in the image of the European Union. Just as Obama's regionalist crusade threatens America's long tradition of local self-rule, so the global governance movement endangers the sovereignty of the United States itself.

Left progressives in America hope to use European-designed

international laws and norms as a backdoor way of imposing their ends on an unwilling American public. With the aid of international laws and standards, the left hopes to advance reforms like race and gender quotas, open immigration, restraints on America's ability to act militarily, and controls on free market capitalism. Obama is highly sympathetic to this movement, as shown by key appointments, such as the State Department legal adviser Harold Koh, the former director of policy planning at State Anne-Marie Slaughter, and the senior director of multilateral affairs for the National Security Council Samantha Power. The president's Libyan intervention was also very much a victory for the global governance movement because it was approved by the United Nations under a new postnational doctrine, instead of by Congress.

The lion's share of the energy behind the global governance movement is supplied by the international left. Wealth redistribution is at the center of the plan. The left hopes to use the mechanisms of the European Union and associated international institutions to transfer wealth between richer and poorer countries within Europe and from the West as a whole to the "Global South."[56]

In his book *Place Matters*, Peter Dreier lays out the logic connecting the regionalist enterprise in America to the global governance movement. He first notes that regionalism can succeed in the United States only with the help of the federal government because any local efforts at redistribution can be sidestepped by people or companies that choose to move. Then Dreier points out that the same barriers to wealth redistribution exist on a global scale. So long as businesses are free to move away from high-taxing social democratic nations to "neoliberal" countries like Britain and the United States, a truly redistributionist system is unworkable.[57]

Dreier's point came to life in late 2011, when British prime minister David Cameron refused to sign on to a new EU treaty that would have imposed heavy costs and controls on the world financial center of London. These EU regulations were an attempt by the more social democratic countries of the Continent to undercut Britain's free market, thereby negating its competitive advantage and spreading the wealth around, so to speak.[58] Here Britain played the role of a reluctant American suburb resisting the demand of its big-city neighbors to join up with a regional government (and be robbed in the process).

Redistributive systems cannot work without inhibiting freedom—the freedom to move and the related freedom of self-rule. The logic of redistribution forces governments to grow larger until there is no place left to escape to. In the end only global control will do. From this "transnational" perspective, the very idea of an independent country, much less of tiny suburban municipalities and states, such as we find in America, is hopelessly outdated.

Obama's redistributive impulses have led him to embrace both the global governance movement and its regionalist counterpart in America. John Wayne individualism is out, and as Obama said back when he first ran for office in 1995, "collective institutions and organizations" are in. A rigorous regime of redistribution is incompatible with liberty, and Obama has clearly made his choice. The American people may not yet understand this, but should the president be reelected, they will surely find out.

CONCLUSION

Reelecting a president is largely a matter of trust. A four-year track record certainly provides a wide array of evidence on which to judge President Obama. Yet freed from the need to face the voters again, a reelected president can move with especial boldness. That prospect has to be taken particularly seriously when the leader in question has promised to fundamentally transform America. We must therefore come to a reasoned judgment not only about what Obama has already done but about what he is likely to do once released from electoral constraint. To make that determination, we'll need to connect Obama's accomplishments to date with an informed judgment about his most cherished values and goals.

Mildly embarrassed by the circumstances of his upbringing in Hawaii, Obama has spent a lifetime repudiating the values and tastes of America's suburban middle class, striving instead to identify with the urban poor. In his eyes, Americans are blind to the price of the freedom and individual enterprise that built the suburbs. Drawing on the teachings of his Alinskyite mentors, a young Obama blamed the plight of the cities on suburban flight, committing himself to what he saw as a Gandhi-like quest to reverse the trend. This is what drew Obama to Jeremiah Wright's attacks on "the pursuit of middleclassness." As set forth in his own words, Obama's life mission is to master the wily ways of "power" and return with that knowledge to help the inner-city poor, whose problems he attributes to the suburbs. The president's political reputation is grounded in the sincerity and presumed continuity of these commitments, as recounted in his celebrated memoir, *Dreams from My Father.*

Obama's actions during the course of his political career, beginning with the years immediately following the publication of *Dreams*, are completely consistent with this early vision. As a board member at the very left-leaning Woods Fund of Chicago, he led an effort to increase funding for community organizers, most especially including his old colleagues from the Gamaliel Foundation, just then embarking on their regionalist crusade. At points Obama was channeling nearly a quarter of the Woods Fund's support for community organizing to his regionalist colleagues. And this funding program was formulated in close consultation with Obama's Gamaliel allies.

Gamaliel's purpose was to run a class warfare campaign of agitation designed to expose the suburban American dream as a product of racism and greed. The ultimate goal was to use a combination of tax redistribution, urban growth boundaries, and low-income housing quotas to effectively abolish the suburbs.

When Gamaliel's shock troops chased the Republican Illinois senate president Pate Philip and bottled him up at his home, frightening and enraging the Republican leader's neighbors in the process, Obama was effectively funding Alinskyite thugs to intimidate his chief legislative opponent. Under Obama's financial sponsorship, his organizing allies knowingly ran a good cop/

bad cop game against the Illinois legislature, with State Senator Obama in the good cop role.

Sympathetic observers of the regionalist movement attribute Obama's rhetoric of hope to his Gamaliel mentors although we know from their own statements that this soothing language was largely a cover for an intentionally polarizing zero-sum strategy of taking from the suburbs to give to the cities.

Obama has maintained close ties to his Gamaliel Foundation mentor Mike Kruglik from his earliest organizing days right through to his presidency. He worked with Kruglik on Gamaliel's regionalist agenda as a U.S. senator, and Kruglik's son served on Obama's Senate staff. Attending Gamaliel's public meetings and coordinating with the group while a U.S. senator, Obama took the partnership between community organizers and public officials to unprecedented heights. As a senator Obama also went to congressional leadership and demanded that a Gamaliel-backed provision be inserted in a bill, citing his special relationship with the group.

Shortly after Obama's presidential inauguration, Kruglik described him as "an organizer at heart," still focused on urban issues and the goals of the regional equity movement yet reluctant to say so for fear of creating a backlash. The key, Kruglik indicated, was to construct a grassroots movement designed to push for urban reform prior to going public with so controversial a plan. Sure enough, once in the White House, Obama went about working with Kruglik to lay the groundwork for a federally backed populist movement aimed at redistributing suburban wealth to the cities and ultimately bringing the suburbs to an end.

The Obama White House has been closely coordinating with Kruglik's group, Building One America, since its founding in 2009. High administration officials, like the White House aides Valerie Jarrett and Pete Rouse and the housing secretary Shaun Donovan, have worked directly with the group, along with numerous less senior appointees. In reality, Building One America is merely a new, less traceable name for the antisuburban crusade long run by Kruglik and Obama's other early mentors at the Gamaliel Foundation, a movement backed by Obama himself since its origins in the mid-nineties. Greg Galluzzo, Gamaliel's founder and the controversial strategist who refined many of Alinsky's techniques of polarization and disguise, has trained Building One America organizers. Indeed the tactics of a BOA-affiliated group in Pennsylvania bear an uncanny resemblance to the Galluzzo playbook.

While Obama's support for Kruglik's group is not technically a secret, it remains a mystery to all but a few Americans. Fewer still understand Kruglik's real goals. Building One America's public recounting of its program is so filled with bland slogans and unfamiliar policy jargon that it is next to impossible for an ordinary reader to decipher. And despite the fact that the regionalist crusade is arguably the issue closest to the president's heart, Obama says virtually nothing about it in public. A single mention in a state of the union address would have been enough to draw public attention. Yet as Kruglik predicted in 2009, the president appears to be intentionally biding his time, keeping the issue below the public's radar screen until the ground for so controversial a battle has been better prepared.

So while the press was coming down hard on Newt Gingrich for calling President Obama a Saul Alinsky radical, Obama was coordinating an audacious policy initiative with his old Alinskyite mentor. What's more, Housing Secretary Donovan has bragged to Kruglik's Alinskyite group that it has a fellow community organizer in the White House. There were actually two community organizers in the Oval Office when Kruglik met there with Obama on July 18, 2011. The day had seen a White House conference on the suburbs, convened at the administration's request and organized by Kruglik's group. If Obama had been meeting in the Oval Office with Bill Ayers or Jeremiah Wright to coordinate a sweeping redistributive plan meant to fundamentally restructure America, the public would be outraged. Yet it's happening now with Obama and Kruglik, and virtually no one knows it.

Much of Obama's own base, to say nothing of independents, would be alienated by the regionalist agenda; this explains the president's reticence. Openness about his antisuburban goals would expose Obama as standing to the left of many supporters. Middle-class African Americans and modestly successful suburbanites now disposed to vote for the president might think twice if they knew what Obama had in store for them.

Kruglik and Obama plan to overcome this liability by splitting the suburbs against themselves, creating an alliance between cities and relatively less well-off inner-ring suburbs. Kruglik has taken the novel step for an Alinskyite organizer of recruiting local political officials and state legislators from inner-ring suburbs into his group, with the aim of checkmating, state by state, those suburbanites whose tax money is wanted for redistribution. It's a risky, highly polarizing class warfare project. Naturally, the president would prefer that it go fully public only after his reelection. Meanwhile he is setting up a federal regulatory framework designed to press states on behalf of the regionalist agenda from above while Kruglik's grassroots movement squeezes state legislators from below.

With little public fanfare, the Obama administration has constructed a daring program in support of the regionalist vision. Even some of the Obama administration's supporters call it a stealth urban policy. Its centerpiece is the Sustainable Communities Initiative, which doles out federal moneys to localities to create regional planning projects. Points are heavily awarded for proposals that advance regional equity.

Once equity boards devoted to redistributive planning have

been established across the country, the administration can condition further aid on state adherence to those plans. Meanwhile Kruglik's grassroots group can fight the redistributive battle locally and in state legislatures, pressing for acceptance of the administration's regionalist demands. Because Kruglik and his top policy people have been quietly advising the Obama administration on how to craft regulations friendly to their cause, the basis for a coordinated attack on America's suburbs has been laid. This round will likely be more effective than the early effort to bottle up Pate Philip in his home, yet it will almost surely include the same sort of hardball tactics. After all these years Obama is still running a good cop/bad cop game with his Alinskyite organizing buddies.

Meanwhile Obama's stealthy effort to impose a national curriculum on the nation's schools is well under way, very arguably in defiance of both the Constitution and the law. With Obama's very left-leaning and controversial former education adviser Linda Darling-Hammond exercising de facto control over much of this effort, we appear to be headed for lower standards, a politicized curriculum, and the end of local school control. Darling-Hammond also has a blueprint for turning the new national education standards to the purposes of the regional equity movement. Common school resource standards would be added to curriculum standards. This would enable Obama to condition receipt of federal funding on the equalization of school spending across municipal lines. Darling-Hammond and her supporters are also calling for federally financed student transfers across districts. Taken together, these measures would effectively begin to merge urban and suburban schools. As a member of the president's Equity and Excellence Education Commission, Darling-Hammond is well placed to bring the goals of the regional equity movement to the administration's education program in a second Obama term.

Obama's stealthy campaign to nationalize America's schools

shows how far and fast a president can move against the federalist system if he so chooses. With the nation's attention focused elsewhere and the states under financial pressure, Obama has used the carrot of federal funds to usurp state and local control of schools. More than forty states have signed on to the administration's national standards initiative, and nobody would have believed that possible just a few years ago.

Keep this example in mind when considering Obama's prospects of forcing regional tax redistribution plans on the states. If federal funding is conditioned on the acceptance of equity plans formulated under the administration's Sustainable Communities Initiative while Kruglik's group runs campaigns in selected legislatures, regional tax base sharing could break through in a couple of states. If state finances remain tight and Obama keeps up the pressure, the dominoes could begin to fall.

On the other hand, it's perfectly possible to envision growing opposition to Obama's redistributive agenda in a second term. As the stealth falls away, Kruglik's crusade goes public, and the president puts his cards on the table, a major national struggle would begin. Recall that Obama's leftist organizing mentors see a polarizing class-based battle as the only way to transform America. Obama's old organizing colleagues would likely see even a losing fight that polarizes the country along class lines as a long-term win, forcing a realignment of American politics sure to rocket the hard-left option to the center of national debate.

It's impossible to tell how far the regionalist agenda might advance in a second Obama term. On the model of Obama's remarkable progress toward creating a national curriculum, we can imagine swift success, especially if states remain economically pressed and the carrot of federal funding looms large. On the other hand, a powerful national backlash against Obama's redistributive moves could bring the entire project to a standstill. Most likely we will see extended national conflict over a more openly advocated redistributive agenda in a second Obama term, with wins and losses on both sides. Whoever prevails, class-based polarization will increase.

To the extent that the president's regionalist crusade succeeds, local control of suburban municipalities will erode and decision making will increasingly rest with federally supported regional bodies that aim to transfer suburban tax money to nearby cities. Suburban school districts will find themselves pressured to accept students from nearby cities, and low-income housing quotas will be imposed on suburban building projects. As suburban residents see increasing amounts of their tax money transferred to cities through regional tax base sharing plans and by state legislatures seeking to equalize local school funding to qualify for federal aid, they will either have to pay more in taxes to maintain the same level of services or see those services deteriorate.

Suburbanites will find it increasingly expensive and inconvenient to commute, with residential parking fees and other duties imposed on drivers and less highway construction as federal money is shifted to urban rail transportation. A veritable symphony of regulations will conspire to coerce suburban commuters out of their cars and, ultimately, back into densely packed urban developments, where it is hoped they will use public transportation instead.

Urban growth boundaries, such as we see in Portland, Oregon, will prevent further suburban development, another way of encouraging would-be American dreamers to remain in or return to the city. Yet Portland's growth boundary and its dense-development regulations designed to discourage driving and press commuters into light rail transportation have rendered housing unaffordable and driven businesses out, hammering the city's economy.[1]

Regionalists like Peter Dreier argue that capital mobility will stop being a problem once the federal government jumps on the regionalist bandwagon. At that point businesses fleeing a regulation-happy town like Portland would have no place left to go. The more likely scenario is that once the antisuburban crusade goes federal, the economy will tank nationwide. The first four years of the Obama administration have been an object lesson in short-circuiting recovery through excessive regulation. Just wait until regionalist regulation and redistribution kick into high gear in a second Obama term. At that point we'll learn that slapping boundaries on geographic growth stifles economic growth as well.

In the end the president would be willing to accept that trade-off. Although he surely would like to see the economy do well enough to keep him popular and in power, redistributionists like Obama are ultimately willing to pay a substantial price in economic growth in return for income equality. Traditionally Americans have rejected that approach, seeing economic growth and the individual initiative that powers it as the keys to individual freedom and prosperity for all. So America's fundamental character will be severely tested in a second Obama term, as the regionalist agenda surfaces. Forewarned is forearmed. It isn't just the suburbs at stake but who we are as a nation.

ACKNOWLEDGMENTS

Thanks are due to Edward Whelan, the president of the Ethics and Public Policy Center, where I am a fellow. The freedom and support I receive from Ed and EPPC are essential to the work that I do. I am also most grateful to the Koret Foundation and Koret's president, Tad Taube, for generous support of my work.

I am particularly indebted to three readers whose advice and encouragement were indispensable assets to this project. Peter Wood is a defender of all that is best in the academy and scourge of all that is not. An accomplished author and astute observer of the political scene, he freely offered his time and advice, improving every part of this book. A poet with a gift for prose, Peter has made me a better writer. Peter Berkowitz, a political philosopher who sees the sublime principles at stake in the foibles of our daily politics, offered correction, insight, and support at every turn. When Peter flags an issue, you had best make changes. Mary Eberstadt blends the music of faith with the acuity of an accomplished social observer. Because she is a professional editor as well as a writer, her assurance that a passage works is as important as her suggested changes.

My agent, Alexander Hoyt, is at once a man of unflagging enthusiasm and worldly savvy. I'm lucky to have him. I'm grateful as well to the entire team at Sentinel, Adrian Zackheim, Will Weisser, Jillian Gray, Julia Batavia, Christine D'Agostini, and Allison McLean, for the confidence they've placed in this work. Jillian's questions, comments, and suggestions invariably resulted in improvements to the manuscript.

NOTES

CHAPTER ONE: ABOLISH THE SUBURBS

1. The July 18, 2011, White House forum was called First Suburbs, Inclusion, Sustainability, and Economic Growth. Accounts can be found at the Building One America (BOA) Web site, "White House Event Report and Follow-up," Paul Scully, July 23, 2011, http://buildingoneamerica.org/content/white-house-event-report; and at the Comm-Org Web site discussion list archive, "Community Organizing and the White House," Friday, September 9, 13:34:22 CDT, 2011, http://comm-org.wisc.edu/pipermail/colist/2011-September/006337.html. A video mélange from BOA's founding summit, featuring an address by Valerie Jarrett, can be found at the BOA Web site, "Building One America Video from 2009 Summit," http://buildingoneamerica.org/content/building-one-america-video-2009-summit. The summit is also described at the Web site of the New Jersey Regional Coalition, "600 Attend Building ONE America Summit in DC, Keynote Address from Valerie Jarrett," http://www.njregionalequity.org/content/600-attend-building-one-america-summit-dc-keynote-address-valerie-jarrett. The picture of Obama together with Kruglik was mounted on the main page of the BOA Web site as of January 3, 2012, http://buildingoneamerica.org/. For Kruglik's early work with Obama, see Stanley Kurtz, *Radical-in-Chief: Barack Obama and the Untold Story of American Socialism* (New York: Threshold, 2010), 95.
2. BOA home page, http://buildingoneamerica.org/.
3. BOA Web site, "About," http://buildingoneamerica.org/content/about.

4. BOA Web site, "Local Elected Leaders Participate in Historic Forum at White House," http://buildingoneamerica.org/content/local-elected-leaders-participate-historic-forum-white-house.

5. Kurtz, *Radical-in-Chief*, 94–97.

6. Ibid., 116–18, 308, 310, 314.

7. Ibid., 93–103.

8. Todd Swanstrom and Brian Banks, "Going Regional: Community-based Regionalism, Transportation, and Local Hiring Agreements," Institute of Urban and Regional Development, Berkeley, University of California, October 2007, 12, http://iurd.berkeley.edu/publications/wp/2007-17.pdf.

9. The unofficial but still important relationship between Building One America and the Gamaliel Foundation is confirmed in "The Poverty and Race Research Action Council 2009 Annual Report," http://www.prrac.org/pdf/2009_annual_report.pdf.

10. Daniel Libit, "The End of Community Organizing in Chicago?," *Chicago Magazine* (April 2011), http://www.chicagomag.com/Chicago-Magazine/April-2011/The-End-of-Community-Organizing-in-Chicago/index.php?cparticle=1&siarticle=0#artanc.

11. Ibid.

12. Robert Kleidman, "Full Participation—Opportunities and Challenges; or How (and Why) I'm an Organizer," position paper for presentation to the session on Collaborative Relationships: Scholars and Community Organizers, Making Connections: Movements and Research in a Global Context, August 19, 2011, 3.

13. For a quick guide to this agenda, see David Rusk, *Inside Game/Outside Game: Winning Strategies for Saving Urban America* (Washington, D.C.: Brookings Institution Press, 1999); David Rusk, *Cities Without Suburbs, 3rd ed.: A Census 2000 Update* (Washington, D.C.: Woodrow Wilson Center Press, 2003). Rusk is a "strategic partner" of Building One America and of the Gamaliel Foundation for years before that. For examples of his agenda's being characterized as an attempt to "abolish the suburbs," see Mickey Kaus, "For Healthier Cities, Abolish the Suburbs," *Commercial Appeal* (Memphis), May 2, 1993; Steve Berg, "Must Suburbs Be Abolished to Save Cities?: Urban Scholar Proposes Provocative Prescription to Address the Crisis in Nation's Inner Cities," *Star Tribune* (Minneapolis), July 11, 1993.

14. For an influential take on this strategy, see the plan laid out by 2008 Obama adviser and leading regionalist thinker Peter Dreier and his coauthors: Peter Dreier, John Mollenkopf, and Todd Swanstrom, *Place Matters: Metropolitics for the Twenty-first Century* (Lawrence: University Press of Kansas, 2004), 276–309.

15. Greg Galluzzo, "Community Organizing and Faith-based Networks," in *Breakthrough Communities*, ed. M. Paloma Pavel (Cambridge: MIT Press, 2009), 231–33.

16. In addition to the case of HUD Secretary Shaun Donovan cited below, see Scully, "White House Event Report"; "First Suburbs Project—Jane Vincent HUD Region 3 Administrator," http://www.youtube.com/watch?v

=oow5MDcH74g; "Building One New Jersey—2010" (video including excerpts from talk by HUD Deputy Secretary Ron Sims), http://www .youtube.com/watch?v=EqL8mmrnzoA.

17. Transportation Equity Network Web site, "April Conference Workshops" (2011), "Morning Workshops," http://transportationequity.org/index .php?option=com_content&view=article&id=407. This workshop schedule gives a brief bio for Kruglik: "(David) Rusk and Kruglik have been working with HUD on how to include equity in the sustainable communities program for the last few years."

18. For a brief, if liberally biased, account, see John Patrick Diggins, *Ronald Reagan: Fate, Freedom, and the Making of History* (New York: W. W. Norton & Co., 2007), 197, 330.

19. Shaun Donovan, "Prepared Remarks of Secretary Shaun Donovan at the Public Meeting of Building One Pennsylvania," States News Service, October 27, 2011; David O'Connor, "Words of HUD Head Hit Home," *Intelligencer Journal* (Lancaster, Pa.), October 27, 2011, http:// lancasteronline.com/article/local/486673_Words-of-HUD-head-hit -home.html.

20. See, for example, Alana Goodman, "Gingrich Revives Old Attack on Obama," Contentions Blog, *Commentary Magazine* (December 1, 2011), http://www.commentarymagazine.com/2011/12/01/gingrich-alinsky -attack-on-obama/.

21. Thomas B. Edsall, "The Future of the Obama Coalition," Campaign Stops Blog, *New York Times*, November 27, 2011, http://campaignstops.blogs .nytimes.com/2011/11/27/the-future-of-the-obama-coalition/.

22. John B. Judis and Ruy Teixeira, *The Emerging Democratic Majority* (New York: Simon & Schuster, 2002).

23. Rusk, *Inside Game*, 333.

24. "Uncovered Video Shows Extreme Coordination Among Obama's Coalition for 'Revolution,' " Breitbart TV, March 26, 2010, http://www.breitbart .tv/uncovered-video-shows-extreme-coordination-among-obamas-coalition- for-revolution/; Mike Kruglik and Rich Stolz, "National Collaboration Drives Transportation Policy," Shelterforce Online, issue no. 103, January– February 1999, http://www.nhi.org/online/issues/103/organize.html.

CHAPTER TWO: MANHATTANIZING AMERICA

1. CNN Newsroom, Transcripts, "Obama Holds Townhall Meeting," aired February 10, 2009, http://transcripts.cnn.com/TRANSCRIPTS/0902/ 10/cnr.05.html.

2. Terence P. Jeffrey, *Control Freaks: 7 Ways Liberals Plan to Ruin Your Life* (Washington, D.C.: Regnery, 2010), 18–20.

3. Ibid., 3–5.

4. Joel Connelly, "As Suburbs Reach Limit, People Are Moving Back to the Cities," *Seattle Post-Intelligencer*, February 4, 2010; Joel Kotkin, "Is Suburbia Doomed? Not So Fast," Joel Kotkin Blog, November 30, 2011, http://www.joelkotkin.com/content/00502-suburbia-doomed -not-so-fast.

5. Kotkin, "Is Suburbia Doomed?"

6. The history of urban policy here and below is largely drawn from Bernard H. Ross and Myron A. Levine, *Urban Politics: Cities and Suburbs in a Global Age, 8th ed.* (Armonk, N.Y.: M. E. Sharpe, 2012), 277–84; Hilary Silver, "Obama's Urban Policy: A Symposium," *City & Community* (March 2010), 1–4, DOI: 10.1111/j.1540-6040.2010.01318.x.

7. Ross and Levine, *Urban Politics*, 280–81.

8. Ibid.

9. Kurtz, *Radical-in-Chief*, 191–260.

10. Silver, "Obama's Urban Policy," 4.

11. Jonathan Alter, *The Promise: President Obama, Year One* (New York: Simon & Schuster, 2010), 131.

12. Robert Rector and Katherine Bradley, "Stimulus Bill Abolishes Welfare Reform and Adds New Welfare Spending," Heritage Foundation, February 11, 2009, http://www.heritage.org/research/reports/2009/02/stimulus -bill-abolishes-welfare-reform-and-adds-new-welfare-spending.

13. Barack Obama, "A Metropolitan Strategy for America's Future," usmayors. org, June 21, 2008, http://www.usmayors.org/pressreleases/uploads/Re marksbyobama.pdf.

14. John M. Broder, "Obama Urges Mayors to Focus on Urban Growth, but Not to Expect Increased Federal Aid," *New York Times*, June 22, 2008, http://www.nytimes.com/2008/06/22/us/politics/22campaign .html.

15. "Remarks by the President at Urban and Metropolitan Policy Roundtable," White House, Office of the Press Secretary, July 13, 2009, http://www .whitehouse.gov/the-press-office/remarks-president-urban-and -metropolitan-roundtable.

16. Silver, "Obama's Urban Policy," 3.

17. Ibid., 3–4.

18. Paul Kantor, "City Futures: Politics, Economic Crisis, and the American Model of Urban Development," *Urban Research & Practice*, 3 (2010): 9, DOI: 10.1080/17535060903534115.

19. Ross and Levine, *Urban Politics*, 277–80.

20. Bruce Katz, "What Comes Next for Our Metro Nation: The New Forces Driving Regionalism," Brookings Metropolitan Policy Program, September 23, 2009, http://www.brookings.edu/~/media/Files/rc/speeches/ 2009/0923_regionalism_katz/0923_regionalism_katz.pdf, 11.

21. Jennifer Bradley and Bruce Katz, "Village Idiocy," *New Republic* (October 8, 2008), http://www.tnr.com/article/urban-policy/village-idiocy.

22. Katz, "What Comes Next," 12.

23. Joel Kotkin, "Bad News for Country Cousins?," *Politico*, March 9, 2009, http://www.politico.com/news/stories/0309/19764.html.

24. Tom Breckenridge, "Policy Shifts Would Help Ohio Prosper, Think Tanks Conclude," *Plain Dealer* (Cleveland, Ohio), February 22, 2010.

25. Scully, "White House Event Report."

26. "Professor Orfield on Office of Urban Affairs Task Force," University of Minnesota, 2010, last modified on April 7, 2011, http://www.law.umn

.edu/eperspectives/spring2010/professor-orfield-on-office-of-urban-af fairs-task-force.

27. For example, Katz spoke at the University of Minnesota, where Orfield is based, and generously evoked Orfield's work and embraced his recommendations: Katz, "What Comes Next," 10, 13.

28. Orfield is a nonresident fellow at Brookings.

29. "Professor Orfield on Office of Urban Affairs Task Force."

30. "Myron Orfield: University of Michigan Taubman College Future of Urbanism," April 15, 2010, http://www.youtube.com/watch?v=JJ30JX-dzDs.

31. Lisa T. Alexander, "The promise and perils of "new regionalist" approaches to sustainable communities," *Fordham Urban Law Journal* 38 (March 1, 2011), retrieved via Nexis, ISSN: 0199-4646.

32. CNN, "Obama Holds Town Meeting."

33. Alexander, "Promise and Perils."

34. Athena Jade Ullah, "A Policy Story of Continuity and Change: Reflections on the Obama Administration's Metropolitan Agenda," Master in City Planning Dissertation, Massachusetts Institute of Technology, September 2011, 94, 101; David Rusk, "Building Sustainable, Inclusive Communities," PRRAC and Building One America, May 2010, http://prrac.org/pdf/SustainableInclusiveCommunities.pdf, 17, 18, 41.

35. Ronald D. Utt, "President Obama's New Plan to Decide Where Americans Live and How They Travel," Heritage Foundation, April 14, 2009, 4, http://s3.amazonaws.com/thf_media/2009/pdf/bg2260.pdf.

36. Corry Buckwalter Berkooz, "Signs of a New Regionalism?," American Planning Association, December 2011, http://www.rpa.org/pdf/APA -Planning-2011-12-Signs-of-New-Regionalism.pdf.

37. Jason Jordan, "HUD Budget: Funding for CDBG, Sustainable Communities, Choice Neighborhoods," APA Policy News for Planners, February 14, 2012, http://blogs.planning.org/policy/2012/02/14/hud-budget-fund ing-for-cdbg-sustainable-communities-choice-neighborhoods/.

38. Rusk, "Building Sustainable, Inclusive Communities," 36–37, 41.

39. Peter Wood, "Sustainability's Third Circle," *Inside Higher Ed*, April 28, 2008, http://www.insidehighered.com/views/2008/04/28/wood.

40. James Delingpole, *Watermelons: The Green Movement's True Colors* (New York: Publius Books, 2011).

41. Rusk, "Building Sustainable, Inclusive Communities," 17–18, 40–41.

42. "Community Organizing and the White House," Friday, September 9, 13:34:22 CDT 2011, http://comm-org.wisc.edu/pipermail/colist/2011-September/006337.html.

43. Kurtz, *Radical-in-Chief*, 202–203, 232–234.

44. My account of the Westchester controversy draws on: Ronald Utt, "HUD's Mandatory Minority Relocation Program," The Heritage Foundation, January 31, 2012, http://www.heritage.org/research/reports/2012/01/ huds-mandatory-minority-relocation-program; Review and Outlook, "Social Engineering in Suburbia," *Wall Street Journal*, September 16, 2011, http://online.wsj.com/article/SB10001424053111904060604576572402 689866500.html.

45. Dana Goldstein, "Shaking Up Suburbia," *The American Prospect*, August 25, 2009, http://prospect.org/article/shaking-suburbia-0.

46. "600 Attend Building One America Summit in DC, Keynote Address from Valerie Jarrett," New Jersey Regional Coalition, http://www.njregio nalequity.org/content/600-attend-building-one-america-summit -dc-keynote-address-valerie-jarrett; "Building One New Jersey–2010," (video including excerpts from talk by HUD Deputy Secretary Ron Sims), http://www.youtube.com/watch?v=EqL8mmrnzoA.

47. "The Poverty and Race Research Action Council 2009 Annual Report," http://www.prrac.org/pdf/2009_annual_report.pdf.

48. Keith Ervin, "Ron Sims Leaves Legacy of Change as He Heads for HUD," *Seattle Times*, February 3, 2009, http://seattletimes.nwsource.com/html/ politics/2008700732_simsmainbar03m.html.

49. Natalie Singer, "Rural Rage Festers in King County," *Seattle Times*, January 25, 2005, http://seattletimes.nwsource.com/html/politics/2008700732 _simsmainbar03m.html.

50. Ibid.

51. "Build One New Jersey: State Planning for Inclusion, Sustainability and Economic Development: Speaker Biographies," http://www.plansmartnj .org/wp-content/uploads/2012/01/Bios_7232010.pdf.

52. Ervin, "Ron Sims Leaves Legacy."

53. Ibid.; Sheryl Verlaine Whitney, "Seeking Sustainable and Inclusive Communities: A King County Case Study," What Works Collaborative, April 2010, http://www.urban.org/uploadedpdf/1001380-king-county-sustain able.pdf.

54. Ervin, "Ron Sims Leaves Legacy."

55. Joel Kotkin, "The War Against Suburbia," *American*, Journal of the American Enterprise Institute (January 21, 2010), http://www.american.com/ archive/2010/january/the-war-against-suburbia.

56. Ibid.

57. Ibid.

58. Ibid.

59. Christopher Swope, "Metro Mojo," *Governing* (August 2008), 19.

CHAPTER THREE: IN UP TO HIS EYEBALLS

1. "Signs of Promise: Stories of Philanthropic Leadership in Advancing Regional and Neighborhood Equity," Funders' Network for Smart Growth and Livable Communities, 2005, 24, http://www.aecf.org/~/media/Pubs /Topics/Community%20Change/Other/SignsofPromiseStoriesofPhilan thropicLeadership/SignsPromise.pdf.

2. Galluzzo, "Community Organizing Through Faith-based Networks."

3. Sean Kirst, "Kruglik on Obama: Bottoms Up," *Post-Standard* (Syracuse), February 20, 2009, http://www.syracuse.com/kirst/index.ssf/2009/02/ kruglik_on_obama_bottoms_up.html.

4. "Strategic Goals 1999 Through 2010: The Rise of Metropolitan Segregation and the Fall of the American Middle Class," Gamaliel in Wisconsin

Web site, http://www.gamalielwi.org/index.php?option=com_content &view=article&id=61&Itemid=18.

5. Galluzzo, "Community Organizing Through Faith-based Networks."

6. "The Gamaliel Foundation," Genesis Web site, http://www.genesisca .org/site/about/the_gamaliel_foundation/.

7. In late 2008 Gamaliel head Gregory A. Galluzzo published an account of President-elect Obama's ties to his organization. The piece, entitled "Gamaliel and the Barack Obama Connection," has since apparently been taken down from the Web but can be found reposted on other sites—for example, Romanticpoet's Weblog, http://romanticpoet.wordpress.com/ 2009/10/12/barack-obama-and-the-gamaliel-foundation-community-action-utilizing-faith-and-saul-alinsky-training/.

8. For a more detailed account of UNO of Chicago and Galluzzo's organizing techniques, see Kurtz, *Radical-in-Chief*, 93–129.

9. Edward McClelland, *Young Mr. Obama: Chicago and the Making of a Black President* (New York: Bloomsbury Press, 2010), 10.

10. David Remnick, *The Bridge: The Life and Rise of Barack Obama* (New York: Knopf, 2010), 138, 180.

11. Ryan Lizza, "The Agitator," *New Republic* (March 19, 2007), http://www .tnr.com/article/the-agitator.

12. Galluzzo, "Gamaliel and the Barack Obama Connection."

13. Jerry Shnay, "Ministers Split over Agency in South Suburbs," *Chicago Tribune*, October 16, 1992; Janita Poe, "Housing Group Hit by Protests," *Chicago Tribune*, January 1, 1993.

14. Poe, "Housing Group."

15. Shnay, "Ministers Split."

16. Eric Fretz, "Practicing Politics in Higher Education: Community Organizing Strategies for the University," *Journal of Higher Education Outreach and Engagement*, 12:2 (2008), 74, 79; Kurtz, *Radical-in-Chief*, 93–129.

17. John B. Judis, "Creation Myth," *New Republic* (September 10, 2008), http://www.tnr.com/article/creation-myth.

18. Remnick, *Bridge*, 162.

19. Robert Kleidman, "Community Organizing and Regionalism," *City & Community*, 3:4 (December 2004), 408.

20. Ibid.

21. Ibid., 409.

22. Harold Henderson, "Up Against the Sprawl," *Chicago Reader* (September 6, 1996), http://heartland.org/sites/all/modules/custom/heartland_mi gration/files/pdfs/5473.pdf.

23. "University of Illinois at Springfield Will Present Discussions of Immigration and Community Organizing," *US Fed News*, April 7, 2008.

24. Manuel Pastor, Jr., Chris Benner, and Martha Matsuoka, *This Could Be the Start of Something Big: How Social Movements for Regional Equity Are Reshaping Metropolitan America* (Ithaca, N.Y.: Cornell University Press, 2009), 16, 172.

25. Ibid., 216–17.

26. Kurtz, *Radical-in-Chief,* 93–129.
27. Julie Quiroz, "Tales from Three Cities: Organizing Race into Regionalism," *Colorlines* (Fall 1999).
28. Dennis A. Jacobsen, *Doing Justice: Congregations and Community Organizing* (Minneapolis: Fortress Press, 2001), 77.
29. Richard A. Chapman, "Demonstrators Chase Philip: Stage Confrontation on School Finances," *Chicago Sun-Times,* March 22, 1997.
30. "1996 Annual Report," Woods Fund of Chicago, 13.
31. Ibid., 20.
32. Ibid.
33. On the composition of the Metropolitan Alliance of Congregations (MAC), see "African American–Immigrant Alliance Building," Kirwan Institute for the Study of Race and Ethnicity, Ohio State University, May 2009, 15, http://www.racialequitytools.org/resourcefiles/grantthomas.pdf.
34. See, for example, the grant to the Northwest Indiana Federation of Interfaith Organizations, "1996 Annual Report," Woods Fund of Chicago, 21.
35. This is counting as support for Gamaliel the grants listed under "Community Organizing," on page 6 of the Woods Fund of Chicago Form 990-PF going to: Alliance of Congregations Transforming the Southside; Developing Communities Project, Inc.; Gamaliel Foundation; Joliet Area Church-based Organized Body; Metropolitan Alliance of Congregations; Northwest Indiana Federation of Interfaith Organizations; and South Suburban Action Conference.
36. Sandra O'Donnell, Yvonne Jeffries, Frank Sanchez, and Pat Selmi, "Evaluation of the Fund's Community Organizing Grant Program," Woods Fund of Chicago, April 1995.
37. "1994 Annual Report," Woods Fund of Chicago, 6; Kurtz, *Radical-in-Chief,* 275–97.
38. O'Donnell et al., "Evaluation of the Fund's," 44–45.
39. "2001 Annual Report," Woods Fund of Chicago, 8–13; Kurtz, *Radical-in-Chief,* 282, 294.
40. Kurtz, *Radical-in-Chief,* 282–83.
41. "Signs of Promise," 26.
42. Swanstrom and Banks, "Going Regional," 12.
43. Ibid.
44. Ibid., 31.
45. Jake Batsell, "Alliance of Congregations Seeks Politicians' Support for Urban America," *Chicago Tribune,* October 20, 1996; Noah Isackson, "Religious Groups Ask Transportation Secretary for Help," Associated Press State and Local Wire, August 12, 1998; Marla Donato, "Bias in Transit Spending Assailed; U.S. Official Meets Inner-City Leaders," *Chicago Tribune,* August 13, 1998.
46. Richard Lacayo et al., "The Brawl over Sprawl," *Time* (March 22, 1999), http://www.time.com/time/magazine/article/0,9171,990488,00.html.
47. Pastor, Benner, and Matsuoka, "Start of Something Big," 5.
48. Ibid., 19.

49. Ibid., 43.
50. Judith Crown, "Rich Burb, Poor Burb: Spread the Wealth: Revenue Sharing: An Idea Whose Time Hasn't Come," *Crain's Chicago Business*, June 16, 1997.
51. Scott A. Bollens, "In Through the Back Door: Social Equity and Regional Governance," *Housing Policy Debate*, 13:4 (2003), 631–57.
52. Ibid., 632.
53. Ibid., 647.
54. Ibid., 649.
55. Kleidman, "Community Organizing and Regionalism," 404.
56. Ibid., 405, 408, 420.
57. Robert Kleidman, "Full Participation—Opportunities and Challenges;" Comm-Org Web site discussion list archive, "Community Organizing and the White House."
58. Batsell, "Alliance of Congregations."
59. Harold Henderson, "The Great Divide: Myron Orfield's Maps Tells Us Much About the Gulf Between the Classes—Maybe More Than the MacArthur Foundation Wants Us to Know," *Chicago Reader* (January 30–February 5, 1997), http://m.chicagoreader.com/chicago/the-great-divide/Content?oid=892581.
60. Ibid.
61. Heidi J. Swarts, *Organizing Urban America: Secular and Faith-based Progressive Movements* (Minneapolis: University of Minnesota Press, 2008), 110–26.
62. The account of the St. Louis campaign here and below is drawn chiefly from Swarts, *Organizing Urban America*; John Sonderegger, "'Urban Sprawl' or 'Urban Choice'?," *St. Louis Post-Dispatch*, October 26, 1997; Dan Mihalopoulos, "Official Calls for Truce in Urban Sprawl Debate; Hearing Focuses on How to Best Manage Growth in the Region," *St. Louis Post-Dispatch*, October 30, 1997; Dan Mihalopoulos, "St. Charles Mayor: Don't Blame Problems on Us; City, Counties Again Clash at Committee Hearings," *St. Louis Post-Dispatch*, October 31, 1997; Editorial, "We're All in This Together; Regionalism," *St. Louis Post-Dispatch*, November 3, 1997.
63. Sonderegger, "'Urban Sprawl' or 'Urban Choice'?"; Editorial, "We're All in This Together."
64. Henderson, "Up Against the Sprawl."
65. Editorial, "We're All in This Together."
66. Mihalopoulos, "Official Calls for Truce."
67. Swarts, *Organizing Urban America*, 121.
68. Ibid., 122.
69. Ibid., 122–26.
70. Rusk, *Inside Game*, 277–90.
71. See, for example, "1996 Annual Report," Woods Fund of Chicago, 21, as well as Woods Fund annual reports in subsequent years.
72. Rusk, *Inside Game*, 282–83.
73. Ibid., 284–89.

74. O'Donnell et al., "Evaluation of the Fund's," 45.
75. Wizinit, "Never Too Old—My Camp Obama Experience or Why I Am Campaigning Again After 42 Years," MYDD, July 11, 2007, http://mydd .com/users/wizinit/posts/never-too-old-my-camp-obama-experience -or-why-i-am-campaigning-again-after-42-years.
76. Jeff Hawkes, "Stumbling Start for 'Bipartisan' Coalition," *Intelligencer-Journal/New Era* (Lancaster, Pa.), October 31, 2011, http://lancasteron line.com/article/local/489278_Stumbling-start-for--bipartisan--coalition .html; John Gouvla, "Wrong Tone for 'Building One,'" *Intelligencer-Journal/New Era* (Lancaster, Pa.), November 25, 2011.
77. Kurtz, *Radical-in-Chief*, 93–129.
78. Rohn Hein, "Testimony Regarding the Funding of Public Schools," Public Hearing Before Joint Legislative Committee on Public School Funding Reform, New Jersey, October 10, 2006, 51, http://slic.njstatelib.org/slic _files/digidocs/s372/s3722006m.pdf.
79. Kleidman, "Full Participation—Opportunities and Challenges."
80. Transportation Equity Network Web site, "April Conference Workshops" (2011), "Morning Workshops," http://transportationequity.org/index .php?option=com_content&view=article&id=407. This workshop schedule gives a brief bio for Kruglik: "(David) Rusk and Kruglik have been working with HUD on how to include equity in the sustainable communities program for the last few years."

CHAPTER FOUR: SAUL ALINSKY RADICAL

1. Lynn Sweet, "South Carolina GOP CNN Debate, Jan. 19, 2012. Transcript," Scoop from Washington Blog (*Chicago Sun-Times*), January 20, 2012, http://blogs.suntimes.com/sweet/2012/01/south_carolina_gop _cnn_debate_.html.
2. C-SPAN, "Newt Gingrich South Carolina Primary Night Speech," YouTube, uploaded by C-SPAN, January 21, 2012, http://www.youtube.com/ watch?v=S2The26NZYI.
3. Jason Horowitz, "Saul Alinsky Lives On in GOP Rhetoric," *Washington Post*, January 23, 2012, http://www.washingtonpost.com/lifestyle/style/ saul-alinsky-lives-on-in-gop-rhetoric/2012/01/23/gIQAXwZ7LQ_story .html.
4. Kevin Liptak, "Who Is Saul Alinsky? A Gingrich Line Explained," CNN Political Ticker, January 22, 2012, http://politicalticker.blogs.cnn.com/ 2012/01/22/who-is-saul-alinsky-a-gingrich-line-explained/.
5. Tim Jones, "Saul Alinsky Rides Again as Gingrich Makes Him Republican Race's Bogeyman," Bloomberg, January 24, 2012, http://www.bloom berg.com/news/2012-01-24/saul-alinsky-rides-again-as-gingrich-makes -him-republican-race-s-bogeyman.html; Brad Knickerbocker, "Who Is Saul Alinsky and Why Is Newt Gingrich So Obsessed with Him?," *Christian Science Monitor*, January 28, 2012, http://www.csmonitor.com/ USA/Politics/The-Vote/2012/0128/Who-is-Saul-Alinsky-and-why-is -Newt-Gingrich-so-obsessed-with-him.
6. Kurtz, *Radical-in-Chief*, 275–97.

7. Sanford D. Horwitt, *Let Them Call Me Rebel: Saul Alinsky, His Life and Legacy* (New York: Random House, 1989), xi.

8. Saul D. Alinsky, *Rules for Radicals: A Pragmatic Primer for Realistic Radicals* (New York: Random House, [1971] 1989).

9. Kleidman, "Community Organizing and Regionalism," 405.

10. Randi Storch, *Red Chicago* (Urbana and Chicago: University of Illinois Press, 2007).

11. Rick Halpern, *Down on the Killing Floor: Black and White Workers in Chicago's Packinghouses, 1904–54* (Urbana and Chicago: University of Illinois Press, 1977), 101; Roy Rosenzweig, "Organizing the Unemployed: The Early Years of the Great Depression, 1929–1933," *Radical America,* 10:4 (July–August 1976), 41; Storch, *Red Chicago,* 107.

12. Steve Nelson, James R. Barrett, and Rob Ruck, *Steve Nelson, American Radical* (Pittsburgh: University of Pittsburgh Press, 1981), 70–87.

13. Ibid., 76.

14. Ibid., 76, 78.

15. Storch, *Red Chicago,* 225; Robert Fisher, *Let the People Decide: Neighborhood Organizing in America,* updated ed. (New York: Twayne Publishers, 1994), 47–48.

16. Studs Terkel, "Sound Recordings of the Studs Terkel Program on WFMT Radio Station, ca. 1950–1999," Chicago Historical Society Research Center, Program ID: T2625, interview with Saul Alinsky, 1962.

17. Marion K. Sanders, "The Professional Radical: Conversations with Saul Alinsky," *Harper's Magazine* (June 1965), 44.

18. Fisher, *Let the People Decide,* 56; Thomas A. Dutton and Dan La Botz, "The Futures of Community Organizing: The Need for a New Political Imaginary—A Working Paper," *Miami University's Center for Community Engagement over-the-Rhine,* February 4, 2008, 4–5.

19. Horwitt, *Rebel,* 39.

20. Ibid., xiv.

21. Sanders, "Professional Radical," 43.

22. Horwitt, *Rebel,* 114.

23. *Playboy* interview, "Saul Alinsky: A Candid Conversation with the Feisty Radical Organizer," *Playboy Magazine* 19:3 (March 1972), 150.

24. Halpern, *Killing Floor,* 156.

25. Sanders, "Professional Radical," 45.

26. Halpern, *Killing Floor,* 125–39.

27. Ibid., 128.

28. Horwitt, *Rebel,* 59–60; Halpern, *Killing Floor,* 113–14, 139, 142; "Herb March," *Social Policy,* 32:3 (Spring 2002), 53.

29. Horwitt, *Rebel,* 60.

30. Ibid., 63.

31. *Playboy* interview, 72.

32. Ibid.

33. Halpern, *Killing Floor,* 130–33.

34. Ibid., 145.

35. Storch, *Red,* 121.

36. Halpern, *Killing Floor*, 152.

37. Dutton and La Botz, "Futures," 5.

38. Saul D. Alinsky, *Reveille for Radicals* (New York: Random House, [1946] 1989).

39. Ibid., 25.

40. Horwitt, *Rebel*, 170–71.

41. Ibid., 172.

42. Robert Fisher, *Let the People Decide: Neighborhood Organizing in America* (Boston: Twayne, 1984), 163. This is an earlier edition of the Fisher book cited above. The two texts differ somewhat.

43. Ryan Lizza, "The Agitator: Barack Obama's Unlikely Political Education," *New Republic* (March 19, 2007), http://www.tnr.com/article/the-agitator.

44. Ibid.

45. De Zutter, "What Makes Obama Run?"

46. Lizza, "The Agitator."

47. David Mendell, *Obama: From Promise to Power* (New York: HarperCollins, 2007).

48. Edward McClelland, *Young Mr. Obama: Chicago and the Making of a Black President* (New York: Bloomsbury Press, 2010), 43.

49. Lizza, "The Agitator."

50. McClelland, *Young Mr. Obama*, 8.

51. Lizza, "The Agitator."

52. Kurtz, *Radical-in-Chief*, 138.

53. Lizza, "The Agitator."

54. Kurtz, *Radical-in-Chief*, 191–259.

55. Kurtz, *Radical-in-Chief*.

56. Ibid.

57. "Gingrich Revives False Alinsky Attack," AttackWatch.com, January 23, 2012, http://www.attackwatch.com/gingrich-revives-false-alinsky-attack/.

58. Kurtz, *Radical-in-Chief*, 93–129.

59. Ibid., 116–18.

60. Casey Bukro, "80 Southeast Side Residents Reject Firm's Offer on Landfill Use," *Chicago Tribune*, February 9, 1988.

61. Kurtz, *Radical-in-Chief*, 112–14.

62. Ibid., 275–97, especially 282–83.

63. Ibid., 293–94.

64. Ibid.

65. Jim Rutenberg, "Behind the War Between White House and Fox," *New York Times*, October 23, 2009, http://www.nytimes.com/2009/10/23/us/politics/23fox.html; "The Obama War Against Fox News: Risky Business?," *Los Angeles Times*, October 19, 2009, http://latimesblogs.latimes.com/washington/2009/10/the-obama-war-against-fox-news-smart-politics-or-risky-business.html; Ruth Marcus, "Obama's Dumb War with Fox News," *Washington Post*'s Post-Partisan Blog, October 19, 2009, http://voices.washingtonpost.com/postpartisan/2009/10/obamas_dumb_war_with_fox_news.html.

66. Judicial Watch Press Room, "Documents Show Obama White House Attacked, Excluded Fox News Channel," Judicial Watch, July 14, 2011,

http://www.judicialwatch.org/press-room/press-releases/documents
-show-obama-white-house-attacked-excluded-fox-news-channel/.

67. Allahpundit, "Obama's Turnout Pitch to Latinos: Get Out There and Punish Your 'Enemies,'" Hot Air Blog, October 25, 2010, http://hotair.com/
archives/2010/10/25/obamas-turnout-pitch-to-latinos-get-out-there-and
-punish-your-enemies/.

68. Scott Johnson, "Obama and Obamism," Powerline Blog, January 23, 2012,
http://www.powerlineblog.com/archives/2012/01/obama-and-obamism
.php.

69. "Welcome to the New Jersey Regional Coalition Capital District Council,"
February 25, 2008, http://cjrecdistrict15meeting.pbworks.com/w/page/
5596209/FrontPage.

70. See chapter 3 of this book.

71. Kurtz, *Radical-in-Chief*, 111–14.

72. Sasha Abramsky, *Inside Obama's Brain* (New York: Penguin, 2009), 20.

73. Horowitz, "Saul Alinsky Lives On"; Bill Moyers and Michael Winship,
"Saul Alinsky, Who?," Huffington Post, February 6, 2012, http://www
.huffingtonpost.com/bill-moyers/saul-alinsky-who_b_1257479.html;
Nicholas Von Hoffman, "Gingrich Is No Saul Alinsky," *Politico*, January
24, 2012, http://www.politico.com/news/stories/0112/71865.html; Me-
linda Hennenberger, "Saul Alinsky Would Be So Disappointed: Obama
Breaks 'Rules for Radicals,'" She the People Blog, *Washington Post*, January 25, 2012, http://www.washingtonpost.com/blogs/she-the-people/
post/saul-alinsky-would-so-disappointed-sotu-breaks-rules-for-radicals/
2012/01/24/gIQAt1cVPQ_blog.html.

74. Whet Moser, "Saul Alinsky Goes Viral Again," *Chicago Magazine* (January
24, 2012), http://www.chicagomag.com/Chicago-Magazine/The-312/
January-2012/Saul-Alinsky-Goes-Viral-Again/; Michael Miner, "Saul
Alinsky, Poster Child," *Chicago Reader* (February 9, 2012), http://www
.chicagoreader.com/chicago/the-connection-between-obama-and-saul
-alinsky/Content?oid=5593347; Richard Adams, "Saul Alinsky: Who Is
He and Why Does Newt Gingrich Keep Mentioning Him?," Richard Adams's Blog, *Guardian*, January 23, 2012, http://www.guardian.co.uk/
world/richard-adams-blog/2012/jan/24/republican-presidential
-nomination-2012-newt-gingrich.

75. Kurtz, *Radical-in-Chief*, 275–97.

76. Michael Kazin, "Saul Alinsky Wasn't Who Newt Gingrich Thinks He
Was," *New Republic* (January 25, 2012), http://www.tnr.com/article/pol-
itics/100030/gingrich-alinsky-saul-newt-catholic-carolina.

77. Christopher Blosser, "Catholic Campaign for Human Development—
Tainted by ACORN or Still Rotten Itself," *American Catholic* (November
25, 2008), http://the-american-catholic.com/2008/11/25/catholic-
campaign-for-human-development-tainted-by-acorn-or-still-rotten-itself/.

78. Lynn Sweet, "Newt Gingrich Takes Page from Saul Alinsky Playbook,"
Scoop from Washington Blog, *Chicago Sun-Times*, January 23, 2012,
http://blogs.suntimes.com/sweet/2012/01/newt_gingrich_takes_page
from.html.

CHAPTER FIVE: A SUBURB OF THE MIND

1. Obama, *Dreams*, 23.
2. Ibid., xiv–xv.
3. The president had passed the ninety golf round mark by the end of 2011. David Jackson, "Obama's Golf: Not like Ike (or Wilson)," *USA Today*, December 30, 2011, http://content.usatoday.com/communities/theoval/post/2011/12/obamas-golf-not-like-ike-or-wilson/1.
4. Obama, *Dreams*, xiv.
5. Ibid., xvi.
6. Ibid., 13.
7. Ibid., 16.
8. Ibid.
9. Ibid., 38. For Obama's account of Lolo's home, see 32–38.
10. Ibid., 29.
11. Ibid., 45.
12. Ibid.
13. Ibid., 46–47.
14. Ibid., 43–47.
15. Ibid., 54.
16. Ibid., 60.
17. Ibid., 55, 57.
18. Ibid., 62.
19. Toby Harnden, "Frank Marshall Davis, Alleged Communist, Was Early Influence on Barack Obama," *Telegraph*, August 22, 2008, http://www.telegraph.co.uk/news/worldnews/barackobama/2601914/Frank-Marshall-Davis-alleged-Communist-was-early-influence-on-Barack-Obama.html.
20. Dudley Randall, " 'Mystery' Poet," *Black World* (January 1974), 38.
21. Ibid.
22. Kathryn Waddell Takara, "The Fire and the Phoenix: Frank Marshall Davis (An American Biography)," Ph.D. dissertation, University of Hawaii, 1993, 372–73.
23. Obama, *Dreams*, 76–77.
24. Frank Marshall Davis, *Black Moods: Collected Poems*, ed. John Edgar Tidwell (Urbana: University of Illinois Press, 2002), xxiv–xxxvii.
25. Kathryn Waddell Takara, "Frank Marshall Davis: A Forgotten Voice in the Chicago Black Renaissance," *Western Journal of Black Studies* 26:4 (2002), 226.
26. Frank Marshall Davis, *Livin' the Blues: Memoirs of a Black Journalist and Poet*, ed. John Edgar Tidwell (Madison: University of Wisconsin Press), xv.
27. Davis, *Black Moods*, xxiii.
28. Harnden, *Telegraph*, "Davis, Alleged Communist."
29. Davis, *Livin'*, 3.
30. Ibid., 4.
31. Ibid., 3.
32. Ibid.
33. Ibid., 4.

34. Ibid.

35. Davis, *Black Moods*, 181–83.

36. Davis, *Livin'*, 130.

37. Davis, *Moods*, 26–27.

38. Ibid., 5–7.

39. Davis, *Livin'*, 112.

40. Ibid., 278, 299, 366.

41. Stu Glauberman and Jerry Burris, *The Dream Begins: How Hawai'i Shaped Barack Obama* (Honolulu: Watermark Publishing, 2008), 113.

42. Obama, *Dreams*, 97.

43. Ibid., 98.

44. Ibid.

45. Ibid., 98–99.

46. Ibid., 99.

47. Ibid., 100.

48. Ibid.

49. Ibid.

50. Ibid., 115.

51. Ibid., 179.

52. Ibid., 273–74.

53. Ibid., 276–79.

54. Ibid., 280.

55. Ibid., 281.

56. Ibid., 283–84.

57. Ibid., 284.

58. Ibid., 285–86.

59. Kurtz, *Radical-in-Chief*, 323–26.

60. "Uncovered Video Shows Extreme Coordination Among Obama's Coalition for 'Revolution,'" Breitbart TV, March 26, 2010, http://www.breitbart.tv/uncovered-video-shows-extreme-coordination-among-obamas-coalition-for-revolution/; "African-American Clergy Commemorate First Anniversary of Hurricanes Katrina and Rita," *Faith in Public Life*, August 23, 2006, http://www.faithinpubliclife.org/newsroom/press/african american_clergy_commemo/.

CHAPTER SIX: REDISTRIBUTION REVOLUTION

1. Alexis de Tocqueville, *Democracy in America*, ed. J. P. Mayer (New York: HarperCollins, 1969 [1966]),536.

2. Ibid., 31–49.

3. Ibid., 278. On Tocqueville and socialism, see Roger Boesche, *The Strange Liberalism of Alexis de Tocqueville* (Ithaca, N.Y.: Cornell University Press, 1987), 133–38.

4. Tocqueville, *Democracy*, 281–82.

5. Ibid., 283.

6. Ibid., 284.

7. Ibid.

8. Obama, *Dreams*, 16. For an extended account of Obama's *Dreams from My Father* and his thoughts on America and the suburbs, see chapter 4 of this book.

9. Katz, "What Comes Next," 15.

10. Tocqueville, *Democracy*, 690–95.

11. David Brooks, *The Paradise Suite: Bobos in Paradise and On Paradise Drive* (New York: Simon & Schuster, 2011 [2000, 2004]).

12. Ibid., 1–13.

13. Ibid., 2–3.

14. Bradley and Katz, "Village Idiocy."

15. Brooks, *Paradise*, 2–3.

16. Ibid., 252.

17. Ibid., 267.

18. Ibid., 255.

19. Robert Bruegmann, *Sprawl: A Compact History* (Chicago: University of Chicago Press, 2005).

20. William A. Schambra, "Philanthropy's Jeremiah Wright Problem," *Chronicle of Philanthropy* (May 12, 2008), http://pcr.hudson.org/index.cfm?fuseaction=publication_details&id=5590.

21. "Signs of Promise," unnumbered front matter (for foundation participation), 24 (for Kruglik quote).

22. Ibid., 3, 4, 7, 8, 35, 116, 120.

23. William A. Schambra et al., "Philanthropy's Jeremiah Wright Problem" (letters to the editor and reply), *Chronicle of Philanthropy*, May 29, 2008, and June 12, 2008, issues.

24. Jeremy Rifkin, *The European Dream: How Europe's Vision of the Future Is Quietly Eclipsing the American Dream* (New York: Penguin, 2005).

25. john a. powell, "Moving Beyond the Isolated Self," Micah Project, April 15, 2011, http://www.micahpico.org/resources?id=0003.

26. Kurtz, *Radical-in-Chief*, 21–92, 299–328.

27. "White House Forum PowerPoints," Building One America, http://buildingoneamerica.org/content/white-house-forum-powerpoints.

28. David Rusk, *Cities Without Suburbs* (Washington, D.C.: Woodrow Wilson Center Press, 1993), xiii–xiv.

29. Ibid.

30. David Rusk, *Cities Without Suburbs: A Census 2000 Update* (Washington, D.C.: Woodrow Wilson Center Press, 2003), 89–91.

31. Ibid., xvi.

32. Ibid., 18, 108–09.

33. Ibid.

34. Ibid.

35. Ibid., 91.

36. Howard Husock, "Let's Break Up the Big Cities," *City Journal* (Winter 1998), http://www.city-journal.org/html/8_1_a2.html.

37. Harold Henderson, "The Great Divide," *Chicago Reader* (January 30–February 5, 1997), http://www.chicagoreader.com/chicago/the-great-divide/Content?oid=892581.

38. Rusk, *Cities Without Suburbs*.

39. Steven Hayward, "Legends of Sprawl," *Policy Review* (September–October 1998), http://www.hoover.org/publications/policy-review/article/7253.
40. Husock, "Let's Break Up."
41. For a good summary of this perspective, see G. Ross Stephens and Nelson Wikstrom, *Metropolitan Government and Governance: Theoretical Perspectives, Empirical Analysis, and the Future* (New York: Oxford University Press, 2000), 105–21. For more on Tiebout, see Husock, "Let's Break Up," and Hayward, "Legends of Sprawl."
42. Stephens and Wikstrom, *Metropolitan Government*.
43. Rusk, *Cities Without Suburbs: 2000 Update*, 135.
44. Ibid., 134.
45. Ibid., 121.
46. "White House Forum PowerPoints."
47. Transportation Equity Network Web site, "April Conference Workshops" (2011), "Morning Workshops," http://transportationequity.org/index.php?option=com_content&view=article&id=407. This workshop schedule gives a brief bio for Kruglik: "(David) Rusk and Kruglik have been working with HUD on how to include equity in the sustainable communities program for the last few years."
48. Rusk, *Inside Game*, 223.
49. Ibid.
50. Ibid., 247.
51. Myron Orfield, *Metropolitics: A Regional Agenda for Community and Stability* (Washington, D.C.: Brookings Institution Press, 1997); Myron Orfield, *American Metropolitics: The New Suburban Reality* (Washington, D.C.: Brookings Institution Press, 2002).
52. Orfield, *Metropolitics*, 62–63; Orfield, *American*, 92.
53. Henderson, "Great Divide."
54. Rusk, *Cities Without Suburbs: 2000 Update*, 48–49.
55. Orfield, *American*, 53.
56. Ibid., 56–57.
57. Ibid., 85–86, 100.
58. Ibid., 57–60, 64, 85–87.
59. Swarts, *Organizing*, 120.
60. Peter Gordon and Harry W. Richardson, "Defending Suburban Sprawl," *Public Interest*, Spring 2000, http://www.nationalaffairs.com/public_interest/detail/defending-suburban-sprawl.
61. Robert Bruegmann, "Density, Not Sprawl, Is the Word of L.A.'s Undoing," *Los Angeles Times*, June 18, 2007, http://www.latimes.com/la-op-dustup18jun18,0,6392240.story.
62. Pastor, Benner, and Matsuoka, *Something Big*, 27.
63. Dreier, Mollenkopf, and Swanstrom, *Place Matters*, 248–49.
64. For more on this, see chapter 3 of this book.
65. Quoted in Orfield, *Metropolitics*, 75.
66. Ibid.
67. Ibid., 75–76.

68. Ibid., 79.
69. Husock, "Let's Break Up."
70. Obama, *Dreams*, 284.
71. "White House Forum PowerPoints."

CHAPTER SEVEN: FOOLED, RULED, AND SCHOOLED

1. For details on Obama and Ayers at the Woods Fund of Chicago, see Kurtz, *Radical-in-Chief*, 291–97.
2. See, for example, support for various groups discussed in chapter 3 of this book itemized in "2001 Annual Report," Woods Fund of Chicago.
3. For a detailed discussion, see Kurtz, *Radical-in-Chief*, 283–90.
4. Ibid.
5. Sam Dillon, "The New Team: Linda Darling-Hammond," *New York Times*, December 2, 2008, http://www.nytimes.com/2008/12/02/us/po litics/02web-darlinghammond.html; David Brooks, "Who Will He Choose?," *New York Times*, December 5, 2008, http://www.nytimes.com /2008/12/05/opinion/05brooks.html.
6. Jim Stergios, "Questioning the Convergence on National Standards," Rock the Schoolhouse Blog, November 21, 2010, http://boston.com/ community/blogs/rock_the_schoolhouse/2010/11/rising_and_converg ing_the_gate.html; Peter Wood, "The Core Between the States," *Chronicle of Higher Education*, Innovations Blog, May 23, 2011, http://chronicle .com/blogs/innovations/the-core-between-the-states/29511; Douglas Holtz-Eakin and Annie Hsiao, "A 'Common' Education Disaster," *Politico*, May 28, 2011; Jim Stergios, "National Standards' Process and Substance Abuse," Rock the Schoolhouse Blog, August 16, 2011, http://boston .com/community/blogs/rock_the_schoolhouse/2011/08/national_stan dards_process_and.html; Tina Korbe, "National Education Standards to Cost the State of Washington $300 Million," Hot Air Blog, December 5, 2011, http://hotair.com/archives/2011/12/05/national-education -standards-to-cost-the-state-of-washington-300-million/.
7. John Leo, "History Standards Trend Rejected," *Sarasota Herald-Tribune*, January 31, 1995, http://news.google.com/newspapers?nid=1755&dat =19950131&id=TikhAAAAIBAJ&sjid=dXwEAAAAIBAJ&pg=56 21,8415932; Lynne V. Cheney, "The National History (Sub)standards," *Wall Street Journal*, October 23, 1995, http://www.aei.org/article/soci ety-and-culture/citizenship/the-national-history-substandards/.
8. Hank De Zutter, "What Makes Obama Run?," *Chicago Reader*, December 7, 1995, http://www.chicagoreader.com/chicago/what-makes-obama-run /Content?oid=889221.
9. Jane Robbins, "Incentives Should Not Be Used to Advance National Curriculum," *The Hill*'s Congress Blog, May 31, 2011, http://thehill.com/blogs /congress-blog/education/163927-incentives-should-not-be-used-to -advance-national-curriculum.
10. Wood, "Core Between," Holtz-Eakin and Hsiao, "'Common' Education Disaster"; Charles Chieppo and Jamie Gass, "Federal Ed Agenda Dumbed Down," *Boston Herald*, August 10, 2011, http://bostonherald.com/news/

opinion/op_ed/view/2011_0810federal_ed_agenda_dumbed_down; Stergios, "National Standards Process and Substance Abuse."

11. Ibid.

12. See the passage from Robbins, "Incentives Should Not Be Used," cited above, and Korbe, "National Education Standards to Cost."

13. Jay Greene, "The Stealth Strategy of National Standards," Jay P. Greene's Blog, August 22, 2011, http://jaypgreene.com/2011/08/22/the-stealth -strategy-of-national-standards/. See also Jay Greene, "Rick Hess Nails National Standards on Their Stealth Strategy," Jay P. Greene Blog, September 6, 2011.

14. James Stergios and Lindsey Burke, "Learning from the Bay State's Mistake," *Daily Caller*, July 25, 2011, http://dailycaller.com/2011/07/25/learn ing-from-massachusettss-mistake/.

15. Robbins, "Incentives Should Not Be Used."

16. Liv Finne, "National Common Core Standards Will Lower the Quality of Instruction in Math, Science and Computer Science and Cost Washington State $300 Million," Washington Policy Center Blog, August 15, 2011, http://www.washingtonpolicy.org/blog/post/national-common-core -standards-will-lower-quality-instruction-math-science-and-computer-sc; Stergios, "National Standards Process and Substance Abuse."

17. Finne, "National Common Core Standards Will Lower."

18. Stergios, "National Standards Process and Substance Abuse."

19. Jim Stergios and Charles Chieppo, "Massachusetts Does It Better," *Wall Street Journal*, April 3, 2010, http://online.wsj.com/article/SB100014240 52702303960604575157753524969156.html; Stergios, "Questioning the Convergence."

20. Stergios and Chieppo, "Massachusetts Does It Better."

21. Alexander Russo, "Uncertainty over Obama Education Advisor," Huffington Post, November 10, 2008; Brooks, "Who Will He Choose?"

22. Bill Ayers, "Obama and Education Reform," Huffington Post, January 2, 2009, http://www.huffingtonpost.com/bill-ayers/obama-and-education -refor_b_154857.html.

23. Linda Darling-Hammond, *The Flat World and Education* (New York: Teachers College Press, 2010), 28.

24. For Darling-Hammond's take on "small schools," see "Redesigning High Schools: What Matters and What Works (10 Features of Good Small Schools)," School Redesign Network at Stanford University, 2002, http:// www.srnleads.org/data/pdfs/10_features.pdf.

25. Linda Darling-Hammond, "Education for Democracy," in *A Light in Dark Times: Maxine Greene and the Unfinished Conversation*, ed. William Ayers and Janet L. Miller (New York: Teachers College Press, 1998), 78–91.

26. Linda Darling-Hammond, Jennifer French, and Silvia Paloma Garcia-Lopez, *Learning to Teach for Social Justice* (New York: Teachers College Press, 2002).

27. Ibid., 9.

28. Ibid., 203.

29. Ibid., 6.
30. Ibid., 9.
31. Ibid., 149–50.
32. Darling-Hammond, *Flat World*, 1–26, especially 22.
33. Ibid., 8.
34. Catherine Gewertz, "New Details Surface About Common Assessments," *Education Week*, January 9, 2012, http://www.edweek.org/ew/articles/2012/01/11/15assess.h31.html; "2020 Vision Roadmap," National Opportunity to Learn Campaign," 54, http://www.otlcampaign.org/sites/default/files/vision-2020/2020-Vision-Report.pdf.
35. Gewertz, "New Details."
36. Ibid.
37. Catherine Gewertz, "Competition Narrowing in 'Race to the Common Test,'" *Education Week*'s Curriculum Matters Blog, April 7, 2010, http://blogs.edweek.org/edweek/curriculum/2010/04/race_to_top_assessment_competi.html.
38. David Foster, "In the Era of the Common Core Standards," Silicon Valley Mathematics Initiative, http://www.svmimac.org/images/Common_Core_State_Standards.pdf; Beth Higbee, "The Partnership for Assessment of Readiness for College and Careers (PARCC) and Smarter Balanced Assessment Consortium: Discussion Points," State Curriculum and Instruction Steering Committee Presentation, March 2011.
39. Gewertz, "Competition Narrowing."
40. "SBAC Weekly Update," Smarter Balanced Assessment Consortium, issue 41, November 11, 2011, http://blogs.edweek.org/edweek/curriculum/2010/04/race_to_top_assessment_competi.html.
41. Linda Darling-Hammond, "Why Is Congress Redlining Our Schools?," *Nation* (January 10, 2012), http://www.thenation.com/article/165575/why-congress-redlining-our-schools.
42. "2020 Vision Roadmap."
43. Ibid., 70.
44. Ibid., 72.
45. See chapter 3 of this book.
46. Amy Yuen, "U.S. Secretary of Education Appoints Darling-Hammond to Equity and Excellence Commission," Stanford University School of Education, February 18, 2011, http://ed.stanford.edu/news/us-secretary-education-appoints-darling-hammond-equity-and-excellence-commission.

CHAPTER EIGHT: OBAMA IN A NEW LIGHT

1. Kurtz, *Radical-in-Chief*, 44–51, 173–74, 197.
2. Peter Dreier and Marshall Ganz, "We Have Hope; Where's the Audacity?," *Washington Post*, August 30, 2009, http://www.washingtonpost.com/wp-dyn/content/article/2009/08/28/AR2009082801817.html?sid=ST2009090403398.
3. Peter Dreier, "[Announce] Harrington Award for 'Place Matters,'" CommOrg List Archives, July 16, 2002, http://comm-org.wisc.edu/pipermail/announce/2002-July/000265.html.

4. Much of the material on Dreier's early career here and below is drawn from Pierre Clavel, *Activists in City Hall: The Progressive Response to the Reagan Era in Boston and Chicago* (Ithaca, N.Y.: Cornell University Press, 2010), 2, 63–64, 66, 68, 75, 84–86, 176–80.

5. Kurtz, *Radical-in-Chief*, 44–51.

6. Ibid., 44–46.

7. Peter Dreier, John Mollenkopf, and Todd Swanstrom, *Place Matters: Metropolitics for the Twenty-first Century*, 2nd ed. rev. (Lawrence: University Press of Kansas, [2000] 2004).

8. Dreier, "Harrington Award for 'Place Matters.'"

9. Pastor, Benner, and Matsuoka, *Start of Something Big*, 28.

10. Peter Dreier, "The Struggle for Our Cities," *Social Policy* 26:4 (June 1, 1996), http://departments.oxy.edu/uepi/publications/struggle_for_our.htm.

11. Dreier, Mollenkopf, and Swanstrom, *Place Matters*, 275.

12. Dreier, "Harrington Award for 'Place Matters.'"

13. Dreier, Mollenkopf, and Swanstrom, *Place Matters*, 308.

14. Ibid., 257.

15. Ibid., 308.

16. Bruce Katz, "Remaking Federalism to Remake the American Economy," Brookings Institution, February 16, 2012, http://www.brookings.edu/papers/2012/0216_federalism_katz.aspx.

17. Ibid., 259.

18. Kurtz, *Radical-in-Chief*, 44–46.

19. Ibid., 35–36.

20. Dreier, Mollenkopf, and Swanstrom, *Place Matters*, 234–36.

21. Ibid., 271.

22. Ibid., 302.

23. Ibid., 277.

24. Dreier, "Struggle for Our Cities."

25. Dreier, Mollenkopf, and Swanstrom, *Place Matters*, 268–69.

26. Dreier, "Struggle for Our Cities."

27. Dreier, Mollenkopf, and Swanstrom, *Place Matters*, 262–265.

28. Ibid., 264.

29. Dreier, "Struggle for Our Cities."

30. Ibid.

31. Steve Gilbert, "Behold ACORN's 'Communist Manifesto,'" Sweetness and Light Blog, October 16, 2008, http://sweetness-light.com/archive/acorn-peoples-platform-socialism-in-a-nutshell.

32. Stern highlighted the exit visa issue in an article critical of ACORN: Sol Stern, "Acorn's Nutty Regime for Cities," *City Journal* (Spring 2003), http://www.city-journal.org/html/13_2_acorns_nutty_regime.html. Dreier and a coauthor then responded in John Atlas and Peter Dreier, "Enraging the Right," Shelterforce Online, (May–June 2003), http://www.nhi.org/online/issues/129/ACORN.html.

33. Steven Greenhouse, "Labor Board Tells Boeing New Factory Breaks Law," *New York Times*, April 20, 2011, http://www.nytimes.com/2011/04/21/business/21boeing.html.

34. John B. Judis, "Labor Intensive: The Most Radical Thing the Obama Administration Has Done," *New Republic* (May 5, 2011), http://www.tnr .com/article/john-judis/magazine/87886/nlrb-boeing-labor-union -chamber-commerce.

35. Review & Outlook, "The NLRB's Boeing Sham," *Wall Street Journal*, December 12, 2011, http://online.wsj.com/article/SB1000142405297020 3833104577070572768248242.html.

36. Dreier, "Struggle for Our Cities": Dreier, Mollenkopf, and Matsuoka, *Place Matters*, 274–75.

37. Barack Obama, *The Audacity of Hope* (New York: Three Rivers Press, 2006), 247.

38. Foon Rhee, "McCain: Joe the Plumber Right About Obama's Socialist Tax Plan," boston.com, October 18, 2008, http://www.boston.com/news/ politics/politicalintelligence/2008/10/mccain_joe_the.html.

39. Lori Montgomery, "Democrats Shift the Definition of 'Rich' in Battle over Taxes," *Washington Post*, October 5, 2011, http://www.washingtonpost .com/business/economy/democrats-shift-the-definition-of-rich-in-battle -over-taxes/2011/10/05/gIQAZj8dOL_story.html.

40. Ben Smith, "Obama on Small-Town Pa.: Clinging to Religion, Guns, Xenophobia," *Politico*, Ben Smith's Blog, April 11, 2008, http://www.polit ico.com/blogs/bensmith/0408/Obama_on_smalltown_PA_Clinging _religion_guns_xenophobia.html.

41. Elizabeth Williamson, "Obama Slams 'Fat Cat' Bankers," *Wall Street Journal*, December 14, 2009, http://online.wsj.com/article/SB1260 73152465089651.html; Dan Eggen and Scott Wilson, "Obama Continues Attack on Chamber of Commerce," October 11, 2010, http://www.washing tonpost.com/wp-dyn/content/article/2010/10/10/AR2010101004009 .html.

42. Kurtz, *Radical-in-Chief*, 39–40, 46–51, 384–86.

43. Montgomery, "Democrats Shift the Definition"; Keith Laing, "Obama Takes Populist Turn with Attacks on Tax Breaks for Corporate Jet Owners," *The Hill*'s Transportation Blog, July 2, 2011, http://thehill.com/ blogs/transportation-report/aviation/169517-obama-takes-populist-turn -with-focus-on-corporate-jets.

44. "Full Text of President Obama's Economic Speech in Osawatomie, Kans.," *Washington Post*, December 6, 2011, http://www.washingtonpost.com/ politics/president-obamas-economic-speech-in-osawatomie-kans/2011/ 12/06/gIQAVhe6ZO_story.html.

45. Mattathias Schwartz, "Pre-occupied: The Origins and Future of Occupy Wall Street," *New Yorker* (November 28, 2011), http://www.newyorker .com/reporting/2011/11/28/111128fa_fact_schwartz.

46. Matthew Continetti, "Anarchy in the U.S.A.," *Weekly Standard* (November 28, 2011), http://www.weeklystandard.com/articles/anarchy-usa_609 222.html?page=1.

47. Stanley Kurtz, "Anti-capitalist Movement Turns Violent," *National Review* Online's Corner Blog, November 3, 2011, http://www.nationalre view.com/corner/282129/anti-capitalist-movement-turns-violent-stanley

-kurtz; Stanley Kurtz, "Occupy Oakland's Violence: Not Just a Fringe," *National Review*'s Corner Blog, November 4, 2011, http://www.nation alreview.com/corner/282269/occupy-oaklands-violence-not-just-fringe -stanley-kurtz; Stanley Kurtz, "Revealing Video of Occupy Oakland Violence," November 4, 2011, http://74.63.51.110/corner/282320/revealing -video-occupy-oakland-violence-stanley-kurtz.

48. Matt Sledge, "Reawakening the Radical Imagination: The Origins of Occupy Wall Street," Huffington Post, November 10, 2011, http://www.huff ingtonpost.com/2011/11/10/occupy-wall-street-origins_n_1083977 .html.

49. The Editors, "Protests and Power: Should Liberals Support Occupy Wall Street?," *New Republic* (October 12, 2011), http://www.tnr.com/article/ politics/magazine/96062/occupy-wall-street-zizek-lewis.

50. "Liberalism and Occupy Wall Street, A Symposium," *New Republic* (October 17, 2011), http://www.tnr.com/article/politics/96296/liberalism -and-occupy-wall-street.

51. For a detailed treatment of the Fawkes symbol from a scholar sympathetic to anarchism, see Lewis Call, "A Is for Anarchy, V Is for Vendetta: Images of Guy Fawkes and the Creation of Postmodern Anarchism," *Anarchist Studies* 16:2 (January 1, 2008), 154–72.

52. John Harwood, "Obama's Tax Policy Targets Rising Sector of His Base: The Affluent," *New York Times*, February 20, 2012, http://www.nytimes .com/2012/02/20/us/politics/obamas-tax-policy-targets-slice-of-his -base-the-affluent.html?pagewanted=all.

53. Grace-Marie Turner, James C. Capretta, Thomas P. Miller, and Robert E. Moffit, *Why Obamacare Is Wrong for America* (New York: HarperCollins, 2011), 145–59.

54. powell and Darling-Hammond on Europe are treated in chapters 6 and 7 of this book. For Katz, see Katz, "What Comes Next," 10, 12, 13, 16.

55. John Fonte, *Sovereignty or Submission: Will Americans Rule Themselves or Be Ruled by Others?* (New York: Encounter Books, 2011).

56. David Rieff, "Saints Go Marching In," *National Interest* (July–August 2011), http://nationalinterest.org/article/saints-go-marching-5442?page =show.

57. Dreier, Mollenkopf, and Matsuoka, *Place Matters*, 253–54.

58. Sarah Lyall and Julia Werdigier, "In Rejecting Treaty, Cameron Is Isolated," *New York Times*, December 9, 2011, http://www.nytimes.com/ 2011/12/10/world/europe/britain-isolated-after-vetoing-euro-zone-pact .html.

CONCLUSION

1. Mark Hemingway, "Insufferable Portland," *Weekly Standard* (March 5, 2012), http://www.weeklystandard.com/articles/insufferable-portland _631919.html.

INDEX